AUDITION MONOLOGUES FOR YOUNG MEN

Selections from Contemporary Works

edited by Gerald Lee Ratliff and
Patrick Rainville Dorn

MERIWETHER PUBLISHING
A division of Pioneer Drama Service, Inc.
Denver, Colorado

Meriwether Publishing
A division of Pioneer Drama Service, Inc.
PO Box 4267
Englewood, CO 80155

www.pioneerdrama.com

Editors: Gerald Lee Ratliff and Patrick Rainville Dorn
Cover design: Devin Watson
Interior design: Lori Conary
Project manager: Karen Bullock

Printed in the United States of America
First Edition

ISBN: 978-1-56608-208-2

Library of Congress Cataloging-in-Publication Data

Names: Ratliff, Gerald Lee, editor. | Dorn, Patrick Rainville, editor.
Title: Audition monologues for young men : selections from contemporary works
   / edited by Gerald Lee Ratliff and Patrick Rainville Dorn.
Description: 1st ed. | Englewood, Colorado : Meriwether Publishing, A
   division of Pioneer Drama Service, Inc., [2016]
Identifiers: LCCN 2016012241 | ISBN 9781566082082 (pbk. : alk. paper)
Subjects: LCSH: Monologues. | Acting--Auditions. | Men--Drama.
Classification: LCC PN2080 .A8855 2016 | DDC 808/.82/45--dc23
LC record available at https://lccn.loc.gov/2016012241

1   2   3   16   17   18

CONTENTS

Chapter 7: Birds of a Feather 123

Chapter 8: Literary and Period 145

Copyright and Performance Rights Information 157

About the Editors 167

Chapter 1:
The Audition
Preparation and Process

Life beats down and crushes the soul,
and art reminds you that you have one.
—*Stella Adler,* The Art of Acting

Preparing for a successful audition involves much more than just a basic understanding of the text, character interpretation, emotional content, and an actor's performance technique. Long before audition notices are posted, the director may have already begun to "see" and "hear" the characters in the text and to think of the audition process as a way to discover actors who most clearly resemble the director's own preconceived images of those characters. In some ways, then, the audition process is similar to an initial job interview. The actor is being asked to perform answers to questions that the director may have about the character.

TYPES OF AUDITIONS

Directors often make most of their judgments about you in the first ten seconds of your performance, so it is crucial that you be familiar with traditional audition etiquette and be prepared for any unexpected audition demands. There are as many different methods of conducting auditions as there are imaginative directors, so you should become familiar with the following types of auditions.

Cold Reading

One or more actors are given a script, scene, or prepared or "set speech" and asked to perform the selection with little or no time for preparation or thought related to character interpretation. Directors use cold readings to determine an actor's immediate skill in phrasing character dialogue and interpretation. Although it may initially be a nerve-wracking experience, with practice most actors can become quite adept at cold readings. The best way to become a seasoned cold reader is to read aloud as often as you can. When you do a cold reading during an audition, do not worry if you stumble over a word or two. The important thing to remember is to stay in character.

Directed Reading

Directed readings are similar to cold readings, except the director gives specific instructions in character dialogue, interpretation, or movement. Both directed readings and improvisation exercises are employed by directors who want to evaluate an actor's spontaneity, flexibility, and ability to follow directions. One-dimensional actors who can only read a line one way, despite directorial suggestions, are quickly identified.

Improvisation

One or more actors are asked to perform impromptu exercises, improv scenes or theatre games. These auditions challenge the imagination and inhibitions of an actor, and show the director how willing an actor is to adapt to unexpected events, whether the actor is a show-off or attention hog, or if the actor is quick thinking, generous, and good at working with others.

Open/Closed Auditions

All actors are welcome and encouraged to attend open auditions, and may sit together in the theatre, watching the entire audition process. Open auditions, often called *general auditions*, can be a kind of "cattle call," where the director simply becomes familiar with the talent pool, without necessarily trying to cast individual roles. Open or general auditions are used to screen actors for more intensive review at a later, more structured audition session. In closed auditions, the actor is alone with the director and production staff, with other auditioners kept outside. Another type of closed audition is "by invitation only."

Prepared Monologues

The actor performs two contrasting memorized monologues— usually two to three minutes each—from classical, Shakespeare, or contemporary plays. Typically, one monologue is dramatic and the other comic in tone. Directors use prepared monologues to determine an actor's ability to clearly distinguish different character attitudes or moods, to identify actors by type for subsequent callbacks, or to evaluate the general level of potential talent available before finalizing an initial production concept. The monologues in this book have been selected to assist actors in finding resources for prepared monologue auditions.

Callbacks

After an initial screening, directors will frequently schedule callback auditions, where select actors will return for further examination prior to casting. Callbacks will be covered later in the chapter.

SELECTING A MONOLOGUE

Too many actors make the mistake of selecting audition monologues because they like the writing, they identify with the character, or the piece is well-known. They forget that the primary objective of an audition is to demonstrate a performance personality capable of achieving the vocal and physical character portrait the director may have in mind. In order for an actor to succeed, the monologue must project a stage presence that is memorable for its creative inventiveness and promote the spirit of the character in an honest, natural, and spontaneous way—in two to three minutes! It is essential to select a monologue that is suitable not only to the actor's talents but also the director's casting needs.

To select audition monologues that may help you make a memorable audition impression and win a positive audition response:

- Suit the monologue to the specific audition call in terms of character type.
- Suit the monologue to the character's mood, attitude, and point of view.
- Avoid performance dialects that are not authentic and well-defined.
- Avoid presenting under-rehearsed monologues that have not been refined through an intensive rehearsal process or actual performance.
- Obtain the acting edition of the entire play, if possible.
- Find contrasting audition monologues that indicate your experience, range, and versatility (verse or prose, serious or comic, classical or contemporary).
- Select a monologue that includes a vivid character portrait highlighting one or more climactic moments, a series of striking turning points, conflict (internal or external), and a range of emotional, intellectual, or psychological qualities.
- Choose a monologue with a beginning, middle, and end—a structured sequence of events that encourages the character to express a definite point of view, develop a clear sense of direction, and pursue a course of action that is ultimately resolved by a climactic incident.
- Do *not* select audition monologues that rely primarily upon costumes, props, set pieces, music, or sound effects to visualize the character. Choose material that reveals your vocal, emotional, and physical range and does not depend on extraneous accessories.
- Do not select a monologue or cutting from the actual play for which you are auditioning, unless permitted by the director.

Look for a monologue that:

- Creates a strong opening tableaux for your audition and helps to frame the character action that follows
- Encourages a personal signature, an immediate identification with the character's given circumstances, mood, or attitude, and a distinct reaction or response to the situation being described
- Enables instinctive acting and bold performance choices
- Has a tempo that underscores the attitude or the mood of the character for its most immediate impact
- Facilitates actions, gestures, and movement to clearly visualize a fresh, original character portrait

A winning monologue is one that feels comfortable for you and that promotes a well-defined use of voice and body similar to your own age and range. Select material that has a conversational tone, which suggests a natural and relaxed sense of your own personality so that the character portrait appears both authentic and believable.

You should make your choice of monologue characters with a burning desire that excites you to perform and share your character portraits at an audition. Always play your character as *I* and act in the present tense so actions and attitudes are fresh and spontaneous. It is important to be concise in both vocal delivery and physical movement to highlight a character's intention or motivation.

SCRIPT ANALYSIS

One of the first steps to take is to read and analyze the entire play. If you hope to create a believable character portrait, it is crucial that you understand a character's changing attitude and mood throughout the play rather than just in an independent monologue. Unless you become familiar with the complex incidents that motivate a character's action, your audition interpretation may fall flat if it lacks sustained continuity and depth.

When you read a script for meaning, paying attention to what a character says and does, a fictional life history should emerge. This background informs your understanding of why a character behaves or speaks in a certain manner. In some scripts, however, the author may include only a few key words to describe a character. The dramatic visualization of a theatre script then depends on your ability to imagine a performance based solely upon a character's words and actions.

Commentary and Criticism

Familiarize yourself with any critical commentary available in the script, reviews, and other sources. Of particular interest would be a discussion of the author's intent, dramatic techniques, character hints, and any biographical or historical references.

The Times

In some instances, it may be helpful to briefly research the life and historical times of an author to gain a better understanding of the world in which they lived. For example, an understanding of Eugene O'Neill's treatment of family would be enriched by knowledge of his hostile and combative relationship with a domineering father, alcoholic brother, and morphine-addicted mother.

Script Title

A script title may suggest the author's point of view or indicate the theme or dominant symbol of a play. Sometimes a title may foreshadow the obstacles a character may struggle with in the script. August Wilson's *Fences*, for example, suggests an image of barriers or restricted spaces that will have to be overcome by the characters.

Character Names

Specific names may indicate a character's attitude or mood and reveal a special role they will play in the script. Arnold Powell's use of symbolic names like Alldad and Baby in *The Death of*

Everymom suggest that the author selected these specific names to imply a parable or allegory related to the impending demise of the family unit.

Character Description

The author's description of a character—either in narrative, parenthetical remarks, or stage directions—will reveal character traits. For example, Tom in Tennessee Williams's *The Glass Menagerie* is referred to as a loner and a dreamer. Tom's purpose in leaving home at the end of the play is to join the Merchant Marine and journey to all the exotic places he has already visited in his dreams. Note what the character says about himself, as well as how he is described by other characters.

Character Imagery

The author's use of imagery—metaphors and similes in particular—to define a character provides an additional dimension of insight to pursue in an audition. A vivid example of imagery that helps to define a character is Tennessee Williams's description of Stanley Kowalski in *A Streetcar Named Desire* as a "brutish beast."

Character Actions

Character is revealed through action. If you chart your character's behavior from first entrance to final exit, you will also be able to identify that character's changing attitude and mood in each scene of the script. For example, in the first entrance of Oscar Wilde's *The Happy Prince*, the whimsical fairy tale prince laments that his heart is made of lead and he cannot choose but to weep. That self-identity then follows the character throughout the script.

Character Moments

Reading for meaning should also isolate significant moments in the character's development or arc. Identifying the ebb and flow of comic or dramatic moments in character conflicts, circumstances, or situations should help your performance build to a more memorable climax in the audition.

Be sure to identify a character's *moment before* the monologue begins. The moment before is that recent emotional, physical, or verbal incident that propels the character—and you—into the monologue. Being able to clearly identify an inciting character moment should provide abundant clues for you to explore as you first react and then respond to the character's emotional or mental state.

Active or Performance Verbs

It may be helpful to define a character's intention or motivation with active or performance verbs that give vocal color to the dialogue, which can help you visualize the conflict described in a monologue. Finding an expressive performance verb that propels your character into the immediate action of the monologue may can also underline the energy and spontaneity of the character's spoken dialogue and physical action. Selective use of expressive active or performance verbs should also help you communicate character subtext more effectively.

Active verbs only surface after a detailed analysis of the character's attitude, mood, and word choice in the complete script. Some examples of active verbs to describe a character's intention or motivation might include: seduce, expose, ridicule, humiliate, avenge, or destroy.

Character Biography

Use the above information to create an imaginary character biography that answers some of the following questions:
- How old is the character?
- What does the character look like?
- What does the character sound like?
- How does the character dress?
- How does the character move?
- What peculiar behaviors or habits does the character exhibit?

REHEARSAL PERIOD

Once the biographical background of the character has been determined, use rehearsal to explore different choices of how you will communicate the character and his speech. Rehearsal should be a risk-free environment to rethink your interpretation, refresh your character portrait, and refine any action or movement described in the monologue. Fill in those blank spaces that may have been left unanswered in reading the complete script, especially any unresolved questions about character intention or motivation.

Analyze word and sentence structure, marking ideal places for taking a breath or adding a pause, and changes in tempo, volume, or intensity. Look up any unfamiliar words and make sure you get their pronunciation right.

Some actors use the rehearsal period to search for a creative metaphor—an implied comparison between the character and something inventive that might give added luster to the character portrait. Other actors use rehearsal time to engage in wordplay with images, phrases, or individual lines of dialogue to orally punctuate a character's spoken language. A few actors use the rehearsal period to visualize action in the script, and then to translate that action into character behavior or movement patterns.

Outlined below are a few rehearsal techniques and theories that many actors rely on to uncover additional layers of character meaning in the rehearsal period.

Read Out Loud

Always read monologues aloud before making character choices. Do you *hear* the character's intellectual conflict, or is it just polite conversation? Do you *see* the character's physical struggle, or is it simply resignation to what has already happened? Do you *feel* the character's emotional anguish, or is it merely sympathetic identification with the circumstances? Do you *sense* the character's climactic resolution of conflict, or is there a noticeable change in character, attitude, and mood?

Units of Action

Units of action are a catalogue of the character's multiple goals and objectives in a particular situation being described by the playwright. They culminate in a *super-objective*, or the character's overarching emotional or intellectual desire. Although generally thought of in terms of defining character in the complete script, isolating the primary motivating forces that drive the character to accomplish fundamental goals and objectives can be invaluable in performing an audition monologue.

The value of using units of action and the super-objective in monologue audition settings is to focus immediate attention on the character's intention or motivation. It is also an opportunity to explore imaginative strategies to realize the character's primary desires. Exploration of units of action and the super-objective in the rehearsal process may reduce the number of character interpretation adjustments or alterations later on.

True to the Text

It is tempting to think that auditioning for a role is primarily an act of performing independently of the play's context, or to mistakenly believe that the whole character is revealed in the audition monologue. Thinking of character as something distinctly separate from the complete script can very easily lead to character confusion and contradiction of the playwright's point of view. Remember that characters are inextricably entwined in a scene, and it is only through their action, intention, and motivation that they distinguish themselves from the other characters in the scene.

Beats

The actor breaks down the script into a series of character intentions or emotional markers called *beats*. A beat begins when a character's intention begins, and ends with its completion or when a dominant emotion evolves, changes, or develops.

Inner Monologue

Inner monologue is what the actor is thinking as the character is speaking. It is similar to *subtext*, the hidden meaning of a character's language. Frequently a person will say one thing and mean something else, or they may be distracted or concealing something.

Objective Memory or Transfer

Stanislavski's technique of objective memory asks an actor to recall the stimuli present during a past emotional incident and then to *re-experience* the stimuli in an interpretation of a similar experience described by the character in the script. An actor can use a specific reference person from a recent life or imaginary experience and project that person's personality onto the character described in the script. This is especially useful if the character in the monologue refers to specific individuals or events.

Critics of object memory argue that it is better for the actor to create an inner life and memories for the character that relate directly to the world of the play, rather than the actor drawing from his own personal experience.

Movement Techniques

Although there is no general agreement in actor training circles which particular movement technique is the most appropriate for character development, there is a considerable range of choices you may wish to consider.

One very popular movement technique designed specifically for actors is the Laban style, detailed in Rudolf Laban's book *The Master of Movement*. This text describes the basic approach of using physical traits and types of body alignment to enrich character development.

Eastern movement styles such as t'ai chi and yoga are highly recommended movement techniques that promote the relaxation and physical conditioning necessary for expressive character development and expression.

A number of university actor training programs also endorse acrobatics, jazz, fencing, tumbling, modern dance, circus techniques, shadow movement, and juggling as effective approaches to character movement.

The more contemporary Alexander Technique, although not specifically a movement exercise, has gained significant support in recent years as a valuable rehearsal method to promote the relaxation and balanced posture critical in promoting character movement styles.

Accents

Use character accents or dialects *only* if they can be voiced with accuracy. Include a catalogue of standard audition accents—British, Cockney, German, Italian, New York/Brooklyn, southern American, Spanish, and midwestern—in your repertoire. It may also be useful to purchase accent and pronunciation guides or learn the phonetic alphabet in order to cultivate dialect authenticity.

Space

Try to rehearse in the designated location before the audition, if possible, to explore the vocal and physical demands of the space. Pay special attention to stage dimensions, entrance and exit doorways, seating arrangement, and acoustics. If you are unable to gain access to the playing space, rehearse in a number of different locations to anticipate later auditions that might be held in a classroom, dance studio, cafeteria, rehearsal hall, or lounge, rather than on a traditional stage.

Business

The role of stage business to advance the storyline or to provide clues to character interpretation is limited in an audition. The most frequent use of stage business calls attention to character behavior or habits and involves handling small props: a newspaper, fountain pen, book, wallet, or lighter, for example. Exhibiting peculiar or repetitive mannerisms—stammering, coughing, cracking knuckles, fidgeting, or yawning—to punctuate a character's attitude, point of view, or state of mind may also be effective stage business, if not exaggerated or used excessively.

Movement

Movement on the stage during an audition is relative to the playing space available. Although movement such as pacing, crossing the stage, etc., may play a significant role in fleshing out character actions in a full-length script, it is less likely to have a meaningful impact on a monologue. The best approach in an audition is to maintain a healthy balance that underlines a character's action, and use movement to accentuate the tempo or rhythm of your audition.

THE AUDITION

It is seldom easy in an audition to overcome the fact that you are basically an actor performing alone in an empty space. That is why it is crucial to create the illusion that you are living within the "stage world" of the monologue character rather than acting on a bare stage or in an empty auditorium. If you have carefully analyzed the script, prepared the character, and rehearsed diligently, you will be able to bring poise, confidence, and total concentration to your audition.

This section takes you step by step through an actual prepared monologue audition. Think of these as "best practices" to introduce yourself in an audition as a more seasoned actor than first impressions might suggest.

Warming Up

Arrive at an audition at least thirty minutes in advance to warm up your voice and body. Regular vocal and physical relaxation exercises are essential ingredients to promote an expressive voice and flexible body. If you have discovered a number of your own relaxation techniques in the rehearsal period, in dance classes, or in physical-education exercises, don't hesitate to use them as part of an audition warm-up routine.

Time

Arrive early for an audition and never arrive late! Check in with the stage manager or the person organizing the audition. If there should be an unexpected emergency that will delay you, it is your professional responsibility to call the theater and inform the staff of the delay. Show common courtesy for your fellow actors by keeping cell phone calls, loud conversations, music, and noise to a minimum.

Time also refers to the minutes allocated for an individual audition performance. Time your monologue and don't forget to allow for a brief introduction, pauses, transitions, and a build to the climax. Don't run over the allotted time limit unless you want to annoy the director and be cut off.

Resumé

If you are asked to submit a photograph and brief resumé at an audition, include a professional photograph, if possible, and a brief summary of major roles performed. The photograph should be a current black-and-white 8" × 10" headshot in an informal, natural pose, with your 8" × 10" performance resumé stapled or attached with rubber cement to the back of the photograph. The resumé includes basic information like your name, address, telephone number, email, height, weight, color of eyes and hair, special performance skills and training, as well as a brief summary of current performance credits.

Entrance and Exit

Both your entrance and exit are part of the audition and need to be handled with poise. As soon as you enter the audition space, seize the moment. Walk with confidence and make direct eye contact with the director, production team, and audience. If you need to move a chair or set up the space, do so quickly and quietly. Then go directly to the space you have chosen to introduce yourself. Don't forget to pause after your introduction. At the end of your audition, pause again to hold the climactic moment of the monologue. Then simply say "Thank you" and exit with the same poise that marked your entrance. Do not comment on your performance, offer apologies, or make excuses.

Introduction

Introduce yourself and the monologue(s) you will be performing. The introduction is a performance in itself, as it is your first entrance on stage and should be marked with a personal signature of self-confidence and poise. Your spoken introduction should be brief, direct, and cordial. A sample audition introduction might simply be, "Hello. My name is Robert L. Jackson and I'll be doing Hamlet's soliloquy 'Hasten thee to thy incestuous sheets, Mother.'" Don't forget to pause between the end of the introduction and the beginning of the transition that sets the scene.

Be Authentic

Your choice of audition monologues should exhibit an emotional or intellectual range that is compatible with your life experience. Select characters whose emotional depth or intellectual curiosity you can immediately define and understand. Honest and simple, rather than slick and polished, are the basic principles of all successful auditions. Strive to live moment-to-moment in your character's brief audition life. Explore monologue characters that exhibit variety in their emotions and overcome significant obstacles in their struggle.

Staging

Anticipate a limited number of audition set pieces—perhaps a single chair, stool, and small table. Do not consider audition monologues that require elaborate set decoration, ramps, or platforms. Stage *blocking*—directed movement in the playing space—should also be limited to focus attention on character intention or motivation in the monologue. The most important element in audition staging is placement in the playing space. Place imaginary characters in the audience at a smart angle downstage center. Perform your monologue in the center of the playing space and try not to look down, back up, turn around, or move upstage unless the script suggests such movement.

Audience

It is not a good idea to use specific audience members to represent a character you may be addressing in a monologue. Offstage focus, however, is a very effective tool in placing characters or incidents out of the playing space in a straight or angled line slightly above the heads of the audience. Offstage focus also places the actor in a full-front position so that subtle facial expressions may be directed toward the audience.

Going Up

Don't be concerned about "going up," or forgetting your lines, during an audition. If you do forget your lines—just go on! You should be prepared by the rehearsal process to paraphrase or to improvise your monologue if you forget the character's exact words. You are the only person with a complete copy of the audition script, so learn to go on as if any momentary lapse is just an integral part of your performance. You can minimize the possibility of lapses with regularly scheduled line-reading rehearsals that focus on good memorization skills. It is also a good idea to review your character's dialogue aloud—in an isolated room or hallway—rather than silently.

Wardrobe

An audition wardrobe is simple and reflects the attitude or mood of the monologue character. The wardrobe should be carefully selected in terms of color, cut, and style. Focus on traditional design principles of line, texture, and modest ornament. Warm and soft colors that complement your eyes and skin tone are particularly effective. Under no circumstances should you wear a theatrical costume to an audition. If your audition includes two contrasting monologues, dress in neutral colors and let performance choices suggest subtle differences in the character portraits.

Makeup

The role of makeup in an audition is simply to accent facial expressions with a hint of color. Men may grow mustaches, beards, or sideburns for period monologues, but the hair should always be nicely shaped and trimmed to suggest the historical period. A warm bronzer may also be appropriate for young men. Do *not* rely on false hair, wigs, or extensions to suggest the historical period, as they are distracting.

Props

Hand props should be limited to objects indicated in the script that are small enough to handle easily without distraction—a letter, watch, pair of glasses, cigarette lighter, or handkerchief, for example. Do not litter the stage with an assortment of hand props that become part of your performance some time later in the audition. It is appropriate in some circumstances to pantomime using props, but make sure the gestures are clear and precise. An audition is never about props or other theatrical accessories, but instead about how *you* fill an empty stage.

Callbacks

If you are called back for final casting consideration, re-read the entire script to review character relationships and interpretations. Do not prepare reactions in advance, and do not anticipate the character or the dialogue you may be asked to perform. You should be prepared for a cold reading, directed reading, improvisational exercise, or theatre games.

Waiting for Good News or Bad

It may take hours or even days before a director is ready to announce or post the cast list. A conscientious director will inform the actor at the time of the audition when the results or cast list will be posted, or when to expect personal notification. Do not contact the director until after that deadline has passed, and it's best to give it some extra time beyond that.

When You Are Cast

If you are cast, it is generally a good policy to accept the role even if it wasn't what you were hoping for. Never bring disappointment or resentment to a first rehearsal. Plan on being as cooperative and helpful as possible.

When You Aren't

If you are not cast, do not take that as a personal rejection. It may be that you simply didn't fit the director's image of the character. Often a director will remember you for future opportunities, and you want that memory to be as positive as possible. Be someone that the director would want to get to know. Do not contact the director to ask what you did wrong or what you might have done differently. If you are confident in your preparation and rehearsal, then begin preparing for the next audition as soon as possible so you may become comfortable, charismatic, and confident. Work towards being a well-disciplined actor who can use creativity and imagination to provide the spark that illuminates a spontaneous, true-to-life character that directors seek and audiences admire.

Monologues

When actors are talking, they are servants of the dramatist. It is what they can show the audience when they are not talking that reveals the fine actor.
—*Sir Cedric Hardwicke*, Let's Pretend

Preparing for an audition involves more than simply selecting a random monologue and memorizing the character's lines. Remember that the audition is an appetizer of your talent, not the full-course meal! The vocal and physical choices you make will suggest not only your potential acting skills, but also your stage personality. Honesty and simplicity are the basic ingredients for all auditions. Explore monologue characters that exhibit some variety in their emotions and overcome significant obstacles in their struggle. Look for monologue characters that suffer emotional anguish or experience a climactic resolution of conflict. Select monologue characters whose emotional depth or intellectual curiosity you can immediately recognize and define.

It is also important that you know and understand a character's changing attitude or mood in the complete storyline, rather than in an isolated monologue. Unless you become familiar with all of the complex incidents that motivate a character's subsequent action, your audition performance may not give significant additional meaning to the character's intention. Some of the monologues in this book are taken from published plays with acting editions, which are the best resources when they are available. An acting edition is a documented chronicle of the script's production history and includes character interpretation clues, stage directions, or character performance hints that surfaced in the rehearsal period or in the public production of the script.

The original and published monologues that follow are copyrighted and are representative of theatre scripts that young men might select as part of the audition process. As part of the initial audition preparation, it would be useful to read the complete script and determine the context in which each monologue is to be played to best reveal the character's intention. Remember that a monologue is a fleeting, intimate glimpse of an individual character in a given moment of time. You must focus that moment directly toward the audience for its most immediate, meaningful impact. When playing each monologue, assume a performance attitude that is concerned with simplicity and subtlety. Concentrate only on the present tense and focus your energy on the detailed character portrait that emerged in the rehearsal period.

There needs to be a strong sense of vocal and physical discipline in your character interpretations that is more than a one-dimensional display of physical or vocal dexterity. Remember that it is detailed and objective observation of human nature that plays the most valuable role in creating honest and truthful character portraits. Remember that, like Hamlet's wise advice to his merry band of players, the primary goal of creating three-dimensional character portraits in an audition is to "hold the mirror up to nature."

Chapter 2:
A Lighter Touch

Directors often require actors to present two prepared monologues: classical and contemporary or serious and comic. This chapter includes comedic monologues that range from amusing to laugh-out-loud funny to over-the-top outrageous.

Select a monologue that is similar in tone or style to the role for which you are auditioning. It doesn't matter if the subject matter is wildly different, as long as the character feels similar.

The actor preparing a comedic monologue needs to put in the same level of preparation and research as with a dramatic monologue. Play the monologue straight, that is, as if your character is not in on the joke and doesn't realize how funny he is. Don't push too hard. Comedy requires a lighter touch.

If you get a laugh, don't smile, laugh along, or break character. Simply pause, wait for the laughter to rise to a peak, and when it begins to wind down, pick up where you left off. Don't jump on a laugh or the audience will stop laughing for fear of missing the next line. If you wait until the laughter dies completely out, however, you'll lose momentum and the monologue could become a dud.

Just as it is important to break a dramatic monologue down into smaller emotional beats, the issue of timing also comes into play with a comedic monologue. Tempo, pauses, and quality of voice can create or kill a comic moment. If there is a punchline, first set it up, then deliver it. If the monologue requires a build to a climax, break the crescendo into clearly defined pieces or moments. Starting at too high of an intensity means there's nowhere for you to go.

If you are performing both comedic and dramatic monologues, consider presenting the serious one first, then the comic. This will demonstrate your ability to go from heavy to light in a moment, and will leave the director feeling impressed *and* happy.

Actor!

By Frederick Stroppel

ACTOR, 20s
From *Actor!* (Samuel French, Inc.)

In this satirical spoof of the acting profession, the unnamed actor is about to give his first performance before a live audience. The actor holds forth with captivating wit punctuated with some good-humored derision of the acting profession. The comic dissection of the theatre and the acting profession is deftly funny. This satirical monologue is unashamedly heart-warming and gives the audience another funny—and twisted—monologue about actors and the acting profession.

An actor? Who respects actors? All they do is make believe. I mean, this is just silly. Look how supremely foolish I appear. And all those parents and teachers out there are supposed to believe I'm from a different time, a different culture, a different world, just because I say so? I just can't take it seriously, I'm sorry. This can't be a man's work, to pose and pretend and... *(Stiffens as if a spotlight has just come on, mimes putting on a crown, strikes a regal pose.)* "I, too, have followed the star to this poor babe's stable." *(Relaxes as if the spotlight has just gone off.)* My God! That was incredible! All alone, just me, in front of all those people. And they were listening! I could feel it! I moved them. Lord, I'm getting chills! I want to do that again! I can't wait till tomorrow! But tomorrow will be better. This was only a surface reading. I have to get under the skin of my character. Who is Gaspar? Was he a tall man, did he stoop? Where did he glom all this frankincense? Did he convert, or was this just a one-time fling? So many questions!

The Bold, the Young, and the Murdered
By Don Zolidis

VALENCIO, 30s
From *The Bold, the Young, and the Murdered* (Playscripts, Inc.)

Valencio, the handsome villain of the soap opera The Bold and the Young, *is explaining his evil plans to the show's hero in a European accent... that occasionally slips into his more natural, high-pitched voice. There is a good blend of satire here. Subtlety is crucial in handling the comic moments. There is no obvious attempt at broad slapstick or physical comedy. Add a little zest, fun, and excitement to your performance so your character portrait emerges as a living and breathing comic character, rather than a stereotypical villain.*

Do you want to know? Sit. And I will explain it to you. It began when I was six. I was a little boy then. My family was poor, my father dressed us up like monkeys and made us dance in the streets. But on my sixth birthday he promised me something. He would take me to a place called the Magic Kingdom in Orlando, *Floreeda.* It sounded magical. Mostly because it had the word magic in its name. So we saved all of our coins, and I danced a little bit harder than ever before, and I made my squeaking noises more realistic than ever, and we saved, and we saved, and soon, we had enough money to begin our journey. On our travels my father made amusing sketches of tourists driving racecars and after only five months, we reached the magic land—*Floreeda.* *(He takes a dramatic stroll.)* Oh, how glorious it looked to me then. The spires of the blue castle, the robot figures of the hall of presidents, the giant chipmunk in a dress. I was in heaven. And that's when I saw him—an enormous rodent the size of my great uncle Supka, an animal so powerful he looked like a god from mythology—made flesh, with saucers for ears and a smile that could swallow the world—he looked right at me, and I was made anew. I followed him—I would have followed that rodent to the edge of the universe, but when he thought no one was looking... *(Chokes up.)* When no one was looking... He. Removed. His. Own. Head. *(He can barely continue.)* His... Head! He was no god! He was a pimply-faced teenager! Right then and there, I dedicated my life to evil. Later that night, I gathered a small group of street urchins and we ambushed the rodent as he was returning to the castle—He was large, but clumsy, and we toppled him quickly, our tiny fists raining blows of rage upon his battered body—when he lost consciousness we tore off his head and held it aloft in triumph—my reign of terror had begun. I spent the next few days stealing purses from old ladies and used the profits to hire a gang of Albanian dock workers—we held Snow White captive for days before they gave in to our demands. Five hundred thousand U.S. Dollars and a plane ticket to Italy. I left my father there to draw sketches and dance his monkey dance. From there it was easy to become overlord of an international crime syndicate. All because of the rodent.

Cheese

By Eric Bogosian

CLERK, late teens, early 20s

News Flash! A clerk at Dunkin' Donuts has just announced a new "Say Cheese" breakfast celebration, and it's an all-you-can-eat special for those times when you're hungry for as much as you can cram down your pie-hole! It's funny, addictive, and delightfully satiric. It's also a darkly comic fable about fast food restaurants and all the health consequences that may follow. Here, we are no longer sure where the over-eating stops and the harsh reality of an eating disorder and obesity begins!

Say, "Cheese!" … Cheese. Delicious, melted cheese. Tangy, flavorful, mouth-watering. Now imagine that delicious cheese smothering your choice of all-white chicken meat, barbecue pork, or shrimp. Then wrap that heavenly concoction in bacon, drench it in a buttery golden batter, and deep-fry it to crisp perfection. What you've got is Dunkin' Donuts's new "Say Cheese" breakfast celebration! And we're not just talking about one kind of cheese, we're talking about *every* kind of cheese! Oh, yeah! Swiss, parmesan, mozzarella, cheddar, gouda, and more. All your favorites. Blended together in a tangy, multicultural, mouth-watering jamboree! Can you imagine the flavor? Cheese that melts in your mouth, meat that sticks to your teeth, and a crispy golden coating that screams, "I want more!" And you can *have* more. Because Dunkin' Donuts new "Say Cheese" breakfast celebration is an all-you-can-eat special breakfast for those times when you're hungry for as much as you can cram down your pie-hole… And all you have to do is say, "Double Down," and we'll throw in your choice of fries, baked beans, or tacos for free! Can you imagine a better way to start your American day? So whaddya say? Why don't you, "Say Cheese!" Get over to Dunkin' Donuts today and get yourself a great breakfast! *(New voice.)* Limited time only. Not available at all stores. Dunkin' Donuts reserves the right to make substitutions in cheese varieties. Not affiliated with any other offers. Not responsible for health consequences, which may include nausea, vomiting, flatulence, heartburn, acid reflux, diarrhea, constipation, incontinence, duodenal and peptic ulcers, arteriosclerosis, dementia, early onset Alzheimer's, cardiac arrest, stroke, Type-2 diabetes, obesity, gross obesity, depression, and death.

Dick

By Robin Rothstein

RICHARD, 20s

Richard, an arrogant, obnoxious, and instantly repulsive waiter, lacks self-awareness and lays all his foolish follies bare. Although he considers himself witty, sophisticated, and persuasive, he is a tedious bore and self-centered disaster waiting to happen. Here he rudely probes into the lives of his customers and makes astonishing leaps of association between the menu specials and his customers' tastes. Although there are some comic moments, the sobering truth is that Richard is an unleashed tsunami of anger, bitterness, and frustration.

Good evening and welcome to *Il Piccolo Castello*. My name is Richard, and I will be your server this evening. So how are ya tonight? You both doin' good? New Year treatin' ya good? Okay. Great. Well, now that we've become acquainted, I would like to take this opportunity to make you aware of the fact that I am not just a waiter. I am actually an aspiring research scientist, and am currently working on my final thesis, which involves lab experiments with rare infectious diseases. Don't worry, I washed my hands before I cut your bread. *(Chuckles, then sneezes. Wipes his nose with his hand.)* Okay. Great. So, we have two specials this evening… in addition to yourselves… which I would like to delineate, at this time. First off, for a mere twenty-two dollars, our talented chef has prepared an awesome seared salmon, which he adorns with a pungent lemon relish and capers, and serves over a bed of sautéed escarole. This special is so a must have! As you probably already know, salmon is not only an excellent source of iodine—a known goiter deterrent—but also contains your cancer-crushing Omega-3 fatty acids. And on top of that, holy cow you get the escarole, which will provide you with the roughage you need for healthy digestion and cohesive bowel movements! Now that's special, huh! *(Pause.)* Okay. Great. So, our other special this evening is a fabulous orecchiette pasta, which in Italian means *(Tugs lightly on one of his earlobes.)* "little ears." The orecchiette is tossed in a tomato cream sauce comprised of prosciutto and hot pepper, and is offered at the bargain price of sixteen dollars. Now, ma'am, you seem as though you're probably in about your second trimester about now, so I would encourage you to stay away from the pasta, considering it does have hot pepper. *(Pause. Listens.)* Oh. Well, I've got great news for you! On the lighter side, I would like to point out that we proudly feature a fabulous steamed vegetable medley over organic risotto, which is conveniently equal to "one bread!" Would either of you care for a nice glass of vino Italiano while you're deciding? Or perhaps a Diet Coke?

Employees Must Wash Hands...
Before Murder

By Don Zolidis

TOROK, 30s
From *Employees Must Wash Hands... Before Murder*
(Playscripts, Inc.)

> *Torok, sleazy under-the-counter manager of a low-end,
> no-frills food court, is a callous, conceited, and unfeeling
> supervisor who indulges all his own excesses at the expense
> of those he supervises. Here, the weasel gives a rare glimpse
> of his corrupt and incompetent corporate management style
> as he conducts an orientation session to introduce a new
> employee to the Burgatorium way of doing business. The
> result is a fascinating and alarming glimpse into the fast
> food market.*

Good. Now, on the Burgatorium team we like to do things
a certain way. Before you do something, ask yourself this
question: Will someone sue me? If the answer to that question is
no, then you go ahead and do it. If the answer to that question is
yes, do it very quietly. And then sign your name to it. And then
sign the form releasing the store from any responsibility. You
got your counters here, this is where we talk to the customers,
and then the customers eat their stuff over there and then run to
the restrooms, which are located on either side of us. Behind the
counter is the kitchen area, which is where the magic happens.
You are gonna start out in the kitchen, and if you can handle
it, you just might move up to the counter. The counter, though,
requires a whole different skill set. Like pressing buttons. And
talking. But most important, listening. Because if you look at
the customers, they just might tell you what they want. And then
you have to press buttons. And talk some more. It's complicated.
A lot of people go to school a long time to learn these skills.
(Pause.) Perhaps this short instructional video will help you

understand the history of Burgatorium. I'm going to go play solitaire on my computer to pass the time and deaden my soul.

Hairball

By Lindsay Price

BRADLEY, age 18
From *Hairball* (Theatrefolk)

> *Bradley, a hyperactive high school student, rushes to visit his guidance counselor to share a tense and absorbing story of having just discovered that his father lost all his hair at the age of twenty-three—and now he needs to know how long until he also loses his hair! Here is a fascinating glimpse into the vulnerability many students face these days as they seek to compete with each other on so many different levels. After some consultation, however, Bradley can once again embrace life with a newfound resolve that he won't be losing all his hair anytime soon.*

Thank you for seeing me on such short notice, Dr. Goodstein. I'm really upset. I didn't know who to turn to and... it's been tearing me up inside! I just want to know... I... How long do I have left? *(Looks up, a little grossed out.)* Dying? Who's thinking about dying? No! Geesh Doc, that's a real downer. *(Looks around to make sure no one is listening, then whispers in horror.)* It's my hair. My hair, my hair, how long do I have left with my hair? I just found out my dad lost his hair at twenty-three. That's five years, man. Five! I know! I know. I thought I was saved, I thought it would all work out. But the horrors don't stop, Doc. Everyone is bald on my mother's side. Great-grandfather, grandfather, uncles, aunts. They've all got the chrome dome, man! Uh, huh. Alopecia. Aunt Betty's bald as a cue ball. I never used to think about my hair. Never gave it a second thought. Wash and go. No conditioner. No special cut. But now I'm running out of time and I'm freaking out. I have treated my hair so bad up to now. I was thinking. I was wondering if it would work. I wanted to get your thoughts on this little idea. If I start treating my hair good, maybe it'll want to stick around. Maybe it won't fall out because it'll be living the high life. I want to give it parties. I want to take it to museums. Take pictures. Be there for my hair. It's gotta make a difference, don't it? It's got to! I'm counting the number of hairs that fall out every day. What's the normal number? Do you know? Is a hundred a day normal? Am I already too late? Am I on my last legs? Am I on a speeding train to becoming a cue ball? Am I going to wake up tomorrow, look in the mirror and see Aunt Betty? *(Drops to his knees.)* Nooooooo! *(Pause. Stands and brushes off his jeans. Takes a deep breath and smiles. All evidence of his trauma is gone.)* Whew. Thanks, Doc. I had to get that out. It was building up inside me like a big old hairball. Had to get it out! I guess I just have to play the cards I've been dealt. And use conditioner. See you later, Doc!

The Hunger

By Steven Korbar

TERRY, mid-teens

In this hilarious comic narrative, Terry, a young man addicted to fast food, experiences an agonizing breakup, then grapples with an aggressive food court employee offering tasty food samples. The confrontation is a free-for-all punctuated with unflagging hysterics, comical outbursts, and satirical confrontations that help to define fast-food chains. It is also a frenetic recital of contemporary character types whose lives revolve around the mall and offers a tart but tasty tidbit of lively wit and biting humor.

After the break up, I just really lost it. I mean, I couldn't sleep. I didn't want to see people. I started missing work. I found the one and only thing that I could truly do without reserve was… eat. I suddenly discovered myself to be an empty, bottomless pit that could be filled only by the pungent catharsis of really junky food. I was ceaseless. My gluttony knew no bounds. Quality was no longer important. It was speed and bulk I was after. I started frequenting the food court at the local mall. It seemed like the perfect place for me—every sixteen feet, the greasiest food of a different nation. I started noticing strangers nervously moving out of my way as I made my rounds, and the foolish few who tried to come between me and my appetite… soon learned to regret it. One day, in a ravenous hurry to make it to Wong's Chopstick Kitchen before they blotted the egg rolls, I passed a Hickory Farms, where a fresh-faced pseudo bumpkin in a checkered shirt and a little tag that read, "Howdy, I'm Jeff," intercepted me and said, straight to my face he said, "Hi, would you like to try our delicious Jack?" The man was offering me free food, I thought. Good food, tasty food, a delicious Jack! Only when I tried it, it wasn't a delicious Jack. It was a mediocre little Gouda! And I had eaten it! Completely ruining my palate for Wong's fabulous foil-wrapped pork! And Jeff didn't care, he just stood there, smiling, in front of that... citadel of cheese! Not caring who he hurt, not caring who he deceived. I took that little tray from him and said, "Now Jeffy, it's your turn to try a sample." Then piece-by-piece, I shoved that entire tray of rancid curd down Farmer Jeffy's throat. After which, I completely lost all control, picked up a nearby brick of cheddar and began throttling him with it while screaming, "Attica, Attica!" I understand now, after this ugly incident, I will be branded with the humiliating stigma of... having assaulted a cheese host. But then I guess most people get a little depressed after a breakup.

I Hate Math

By Connie Schindewolf

STUDENT, age 15

A precocious ninth grade student tries to sum up for his advisor the more or less indescribable: why he hates math class! His reason is that his low-brow, low-life hoodlum classmates cause constant commotion and destroy instructional supplies. The atmosphere is bleak in this discomforting and sometimes outright agonizing learning environment. The events, however, are treated with lively wit and biting humor that builds toward a thoroughly delightful climax.

I hate math! No, I mean I really hate math! The class that is… 9th grade regular math. Huh, there's nothing regular about it. It's the most irregular class you could ever imagine… for dummies. Actually, I'm not a dummy. I'm gifted in language arts. I think it's 'cause my parents taught me to read at like two, yeah, that's right, two! They put those little magnetic letters on the fridge and taught me to read my name before I could walk. If only they would have started on the math a little earlier. I mean, I think I've just convinced myself I suck at it… 'cause I'm not stupid, really. But now I'm doomed… no chance of ever getting into an advanced math class. As easy as it is, I'm still getting C's and D's 'cause nothing goes on in there, except these lowlifes tearing the place up. I mean it. The poor teacher's been through like fifteen pencil sharpeners. When we're supposed to be dividing fractions, these future inmates are breaking their lead on purpose so they can get out of their seats and cause a commotion. I mean, nothing gets done. If she doesn't hear a swear word all period, we get a piece of candy. Can you believe it? I get sick to my stomach just walking to math class 'cause I know what's coming. I just sit there and never say anything. One time I gave one of the kids a dirty look when he threw something at the teacher, and he said to me, "Your sister's real cute. And I know where you live." So, I just sit there and never say anything and watch the poor teacher with her tons of paperwork and stacks of office referrals, which never do any good anyway. God, I hate math!

I Know What the Guy Eats for Breakfast

By Leigh Podgorski

DEITER, 20s

From *Amara*

Deiter Olbrych, an overly dramatic young actor who is unabashedly vain, would test any director's patience with his unbridled assertiveness. Here he confronts a playwright about rewrites for his character Johnny Jakes in the script Dance with Death. Deiter's zeal in playing blood-and-guts fiction stage characters, however, is frequently accentuated with unintentional comic undertones. This may lead you to wonder if Deiter's real-life role is acted out with the same carefree spirit and sense of abandon.

Eva! Eva! There you are! I've been looking all over for you. Have you got the rewrites? Gwynne told me you were going to change the ending. That now, instead of Johnny slicing Mary open with a knife, he's going to smash her brains out with the fire poker. Oh, God, Eva, that's brilliant. Absolutely brilliant playwriting. I mean, the whole piece is brilliant, of course. What else could it be? I think it's going to make my career, actually, but this latest idea, this is absolutely smashing. What took you so long to come up with it? *(Pause.)* No, no, I understand. I mean, writing a play. I could never even attempt it. Well, maybe I could. But the fire poker. Wow. That's exactly who Johnny Jakes is. Savage. Wild. Out of control. When Gwynne told me you were going to change the ending, Eva, I was so excited I couldn't sleep. All last night, I tossed and turned, the images just flying at me so fast, I couldn't stop them. I couldn't turn them off. God! What drama! Picture it! The stage, splattered with blood. Me, splattered with blood. I enter for my curtain call, exhausted, spent, covered with blood. I bow. Barely able to move from the exhaustion. The crowd goes wild. Oh, Eva, Johnny has just got to bludgeon Mary to death with that fire poker. Gwynne promised me you would change the ending. I know how these things work. I know the theatre. I know drama. You give me a character, any character, and I'll make him fly. I've proved it with Johnny Jakes, haven't I? Oh, I'd make a devastating playwright, if I could ever find the time to just sit down and do it. Eva, I know who Johnny Jakes is. I know how he thinks. I know what he feels. Christ, Eva, I know what the guy eats for breakfast. He has got to smash Mary's brains out with that fire poker. That's the only way the play will work. That's the only way Johnny Jakes would kill.

New Action Army

By Eric Bogosian

RECRUITER, 30s or 40s

A recruiter for the New Action Army has just announced a new enlistment call to encourage young men to learn a skill, wear a free uniform, meet a bunch of great guys, and even earn a little money! Looking for modern day heroes, the New Action Army is a beacon to those struggling to make the world a better place and offers a powerful incentive to those with moral courage to come and be part of it. Although there is a slightly irreverent tone to the monologue, the dialogue is truly a hilarious send-up of professional organizations and their recruiting tactics.

Hey! Can I ask you a question? Are you a confused young guy? Don't know where you're going? Can't find a job? Lonely? I may have the answer for you. But first let me ask you this. How'd you like to have a job where you travel all over the world? A job where you learn a skill, wear a free uniform, meet a bunch of great guys and even earn a little money? If your answer is "Yes!" You might be the kind of guy we're looking for in the NEW ACTION ARMY. How'd you like to handle a lethal weapon? Work with explosives? Be feared and even hated by everyone you meet? Get to know real prostitutes? PLUS wear a uniform that's recognized (and respected) just about everywhere... while you hang out with a bunch of great guys who like to have fun, play cards, and drink? And how 'bout the excitement? You think bungee jumping is fun? You like roller coasters? How about putting your life on the line twenty-four hours a day! That's excitement. You can't beat it. And if you do get injured you can be sure of one thing. We'll be there to support you with the best medical care (and cool meds!) money can buy! So whaddya say? The army's a lotta fun! Come on and be a part of it! The New Action Army—Where the Action Is!

Till We Meet Again

By Colin and Mary Crowther

TEENAGER, early teens
From *Till We Meet Again* (Samuel French Ltd.)

In this increasingly frenetic—and funny—self-portrait of a bewildered teenager coming to grips with the frustrations and perils of daily life, we have an explosively funny depiction of adolescent angst and anxiety! The teenager wants to take responsibility for his life, but finds himself temporarily immobile and unable to appreciate the good times. Although ignoring all the disturbing issues in his life, the teenager offers a touching and very perceptive examination of adolescent courage and the infinite varieties of teenage angst.

Oh, no! It's happening again. I'm sweating. Do you know the first thing I'll do? When I know everything? I'll invent a cure for puberty. No more flushes and blushes and gallons of sweat and stink and… things. I'll be able to say, "You are my body and you are under my control. You are my brain and you will think what I tell you, and when I tell you, and you will never embarrass me on public transport again!" And when someone says—oh, something clever and cutting—I'll be able to come back with just the right words. Kapow! And I'll be smooth and cool and… and not sweaty and sticky and covered in zits! Do you know my greatest fear? That one day someone will squeeze me—and I'm so oily and sweaty and sticky—I'll just go pffft and pop out of my shirt—my whole body will pop out of my clothes and up in the air and I'll be up there in full view of everyone— stark bollock naked—and they'll all laugh! Because they don't understand. No one understands… what it's like… to be me!

The Vandal

By Hamish Linklater

BOY, early teens
From *The Vandal* (Dramatists Play Service, Inc.)

On a cold winter night in Kingston, New York, a teenage boy and an older woman meet at a bus stop surrounded by a hospital, a cemetery, and a liquor store. The bus stop functions as a kind of limbo, a meeting place for lost souls. Although the woman listens intently to the boy's conversation, she is unable to translate his metaphors or mystic images into flesh-and-blood thoughts that make rational sense. Later, it is revealed that the boy died more than a year ago in a horrible car accident and the improbable meeting takes on an air of the supernatural.

You know what I like with Cool Ranch, any Dorito really, as opposed to like a Sun Chip? Or a... I don't know, regular tortilla chip? The flavor dust that gets stuck to your fingers when you bite your chip. See? With Cool Ranch, it's like a blue and gold flavor dust. It's not really the color of ranch dressing. Maybe it's a metaphor. "Cool Ranch..." But then look at this... so like, you lick it off. The flavor dust. *(Licks his fingers.)* Voila. But then when you go for the next chip, your fingers are like wet and sticky, so more flavor dust sticks to your fingers, so you lick 'em again, and your fingers get wetter and stickier, so there's gonna be more flavor dust, there's gonna be more licking, and eventually it'll just coat your fingers. Your tongue and lips get coated too, and who knows eventually if the licking is actually cleaning your fingers, or just shellacking on more layers of pasty flavor dust. It's just like this passing back and forth of smoosh that's losing flavor. It's just this cleaning which isn't even tasting anymore, this cleaning that's only making a bigger mess. It's a negative feedback cycle. And the chip, the start of the whole thing, is like beside the point. Do you think that's a metaphor?

Chapter 3:
Guilt and Regret

The monologues in this chapter are dramatic, rather than tragic. Filled with remorse, regret, and sometimes shame, these speeches require commitment and authenticity in their performance, but do not demand the same emotional price of those in the tragedy and trauma chapter. They are more about pathos than horror. The characters explain rather than relive past events and address the consequences, which, while serious, are not necessarily dire.

You might think these characters are somewhat unremarkable compared to those in other chapters. Despite their ordinary appearances, all of them have a lesson they have learned, a point to make, and a chance to turn things around for the better.

Be careful not to force large emotions in these monologues. Speak candidly and let the text tell the story. In most cases, you will be trying to elicit sympathy for the character, not to alienate the director with histrionics. These kinds of characters often appear in supporting roles in dramas.

All Good Children Go to Heaven

By M.E.H. Lewis and Barbara Lhota

STOLI, age 17
From *All Good Children Go to Heaven*

> *Stoli is a sensitive seventeen-year-old foster child from a*
> *broken home who was unceremoniously abandoned by his*
> *mother. He recounts the detailed and emotionally shattering*
> *experience that has left him embittered.*

They're good to us here. I don't want them to hate me like
my mother. *(Pause.)* She does. Hate me. My mother sent me
because she said she had to get her head clear. I was fourteen
and she said there was too much going on, so I was going to
stay with my aunt in Chicago. "It'll be an adventure, Stoli," she
said. "You get to see the big city." She gave me some peanut
butter sandwiches and a bag of Doritos to eat on the way. She
pinned a twenty dollar bill and my auntie's address inside my
jacket, and said, "Make sure you don't lose those." So I rode
the bus six hours from Indy. And I figured out the El system
with all those colors and took the Red Line to the address Mom
gave me. But there's no houses on the street, just a taco place.
And they never heard of my aunt. I called my mom, but she
wouldn't answer. I slept in a tree by the beach. Figured being up
high would be safer and nobody would see me. Every day I'm
calling my mom but there's no answer, and I'm sleeping in the
trees, and there's nothing left to eat but Dorito crumbs. The taco
guy must have felt sorry for me, because he gave me some beans
and rice. I keep calling and calling, and finally she answers.
She said, "Stoli, I can't take care of you anymore. I gotta get
my head clear. Chicago's got real good social services. You go
get some help. You'll be okay." And then she just hung up. She
never answered again, no matter how many times I called.

Aposiopesis*

By John P. McEneny

MARCEL, age 23
From *Aposiopesis*

> *It is a brisk fall afternoon on the quad at Saddlewood College and Marcel, a frazzled young man, is being followed by a small but abrasive and petulant girl named Beth Looper. They are both romantic literature majors—but no longer romantically involved with each other. Marcel now takes this fleeting opportunity to address his bitterness of the past and confront the hard-driving and relentless Beth in vivid language that is sharply critical and incisive—finally signaling that this is the ultimate disintegration of their relationship.*

Lower your voice. I was not playing with Elina Plugaru's ponytail during the lecture. I was not stroking it. I was barely petting it. It was just there. Dangling freely on my desk while I'm taking notes. What the hell am I supposed to do? Who are you to judge me? Why are you even watching me? Beth!? Beth. NO! NO! What do you even care what I do with Elina Plugaru's hair? You're not my girlfriend. You had your chance one year ago at Model Congress and you blew it, lady! And don't pretend you were drunk on wine coolers because the stuff you said was really cruel and small and unforgivable. And it wasn't a perm— it was a relaxer. Many men use it. I told you—my cousin Manny mixed the ammonium thioglycolate with too much petroleum jelly and then left it in too long… and he should have used a neutralizer and just shut up. NO! Maybe I was just trying to look nice for you. *(Pause.)* That night at the Comfort Lodge was really important to me. It was supposed to have been special and it took a lot of planning on my part. I was very vulnerable and you knew it. It may not have been your first time but it was mine and I wanted it to be nice. And you ruined it. I had to borrow money from my dad. I had to pay almost three-hundred dollars for a new ozonator because the rose petals got stuck in the filter of the jacuzzi. I had to borrow money from my dad. Try lying to your dad that you were at a Comfort Inn ALONE on a Tuesday night in a jacuzzi filled with rose petals. He still won't look at me. It doesn't matter anymore. I'm happy now. Now finally I'm happy and I don't think about you anymore. I feel good about myself, and my hair is growing in, and I'm happy, and I aced my G.R.E.s and now... NOW, you're acting like a scorned woman? Like you're Nastasya Filippovna from that stupid Dostoyevsky novel. If you think you're going to bring your jealousy and misplaced romantic aspirations into literary journal then you're dead wrong. You're not ruining my senior year, Beth.

To be silent or a sudden breaking off of a thought in the middle of a sentence as if one were unable or unwilling to continue.

Basketball Champ

By Steven Fendrich

TIM, age 17
From *Yearbook* (Pioneer Drama Service)

> *Tim is a dedicated and popular high school athlete who is under pressure to impress both his father and his coach, and carry the team to victory. With seconds left in the game, all eyes are on him as he stands at the free throw line, and everything is at stake. Will he triumph or choke? This monologue explores how a single moment of success or failure can redefine a young person's relationships and dreams.*

(Mimes holding a basketball.) I'll see you after the game, Dad. *(To audience.)* What a game it was. I swear the score went back and forth a million times. I had to play up against this one guy who must have been six inches taller than me. This guy was big… and strong! I can remember how exhausted I was just guarding this guy. Man, what a game! It sure went fast! It seems every time I would blink, a quarter would be over. And even though I thought we should have been up by twenty, the score was always even. But Coach kept me in because I had a hot hand that night. I mean, that was truly my night! I was able to get off some good shots… and the lucky ones were falling in, too. But the Panthers were doing great. Every shot we would make, they would come back and match it. When they went up by one with just five seconds left, we called time-out. The plan was for me to get the ball and go to the basket. *(Mimes bouncing the ball.)* So, as soon as I touched the ball, I took it fast to the hoop. *(Runs toward imaginary basket.)* I went up and the big guy hit me on the arm. With the place screaming, I didn't even hear a whistle. I sort of remember the cheers, I guess. All I know is that my head was spinning. The ref handed me the ball and told me I had two shots. The other team called a time-out just to get my mind

working too much. But Coach was great. He had confidence in me, and I believed him. This was my time. You know, the minutes of fame everyone always talks about. My teammates were yelling and slapping me on the back. Yeah, my head was spinning. But after all, I was the best shooter on my team, and like Dad said, I'd been carrying my team. Who could doubt that this was the moment I'd been waiting for all my life. You see, this was living the dream. When you grow up being a jock like me, you dream of hitting the home run in the bottom of the ninth to win the World Series, catching the touchdown pass to win the Super Bowl or… sinking the shot to win the state championship. I was actually living my dream! So I knew I would win it all. I stepped up to the foul line… *(Mimes bouncing ball three times and looks at "basket," ready to shoot.)* I wiped off the sweat that was dripping from my forehead. *(Wipes forehead.)* I bounced the ball three times. You see, I always bounce the ball three times before a foul shot. *(Pause.)* Okay. This is it. This is fame. In a few seconds I'll be cutting the net. Fans will be mauling me, carrying me off of the court. And Dad. So I took a deep breath. *(Deep breath.)* And shot. *(Misses.)* Okay. Okay. Okay. No problem. I'll send it into overtime and then win it for the team. But what did I just do wrong? My dream is out-of-sync. There are my teammates. *(Looks UPSTAGE.)* They're so nervous they can't even look up. Okay. Let's just send it into overtime. Three times. *(Mimes bouncing ball three times.)* Deep breath. *(Takes breath.)* And… *(Shoots. Whether TIM made it or not is unclear.)* I can't believe it! *(He falls to the ground and pounds his fist on floor.)* I blew it! I blew it! I blew it! *(Looks up from the floor. Gets up.)* And there's Dad. I don't want to look him in the eyes. Wasn't this his moment, too? Isn't this what a father dreams about? What he tells his friends about for years to come? And now I have to face him. I've let him down. *(Long pause.)* I screwed up, Dad. I blew it. I missed it. I'm sorry. Really. I'm sorry.

Bring Back Peter Paul Rubens

By Barbara Lhota and Janet B. Milstein

JERRY, late 20s

Jerry, an emotionally fragile and vulnerable young man, was frustrated with his lot in high school. He had serious emotional problems while trying to come to terms with being overweight. Although answers to the main question of his youth—Why was I like I was?—weren't forthcoming, Jerry struggled valiantly to make sense of his childhood. Now he shares with his wife an incident that helped him decide that his only hope to rid himself of this burden was to lose weight.

Okay… when my father died, I started gaining weight. I mean, right when he died. Everybody and their brother kept bringing all this food to us. It's what people do. I don't know why. It's not like food would make up for my dad being gone. My dad was dead, but we had pies and cakes falling off our counters. I was always real confident before that, too. My mother didn't want to talk about my father's death. Every time I brought it up, she'd invite me to sit down and eat. It was like it was supposed to make me feel better or something. And it did in the moment— until afterwards. It was kind of an obsession. Like keeping me connected to my dad. Before I knew it, I had put on fifty pounds. I couldn't believe it. I'd suddenly become… fat. I was dating this girl, Samantha, at the time. We were in gym class one day. We had one of those stupid rope things. I couldn't get up at all. I just kept slipping. My hands were all raw and burnt. And I was sweating like crazy. That never happened before. I was always pretty good in gym. And then these guys started laughing at me. Then they started cracking jokes about how fat I was. One of them turned to Samantha and oinked. He just kept oinking over and over. "It must be fun doing it with a pig! I'm amazed he hasn't squashed you yet." And then they all burst out laughing.

Samantha broke up with me that very same day. She couldn't even look me in the face.

The Emerald Circle

By Max Bush

DAVE, age 14
From *The Emerald Circle* (Dramatic Publishing Co.)

Dave, a sensitive young teenager with an explosive temper,
started a fist fight without any provocation with his best
friend, Chris, during a backyard basketball game. Chris
recognizes Dave's explosive behavior as an emotional cry
for help and—above all else—a desperate need to reveal the
honest truth of a recent violent attack he experienced with
his girlfriend. This probing character sketch recognizes the
power of courage over fear, and ultimately reaffirms the true
nature of friendship.

I keep seeing that night over and over again. I hear him. It's like
he's right here, right next to me, talking to me, talking. I can't
shut him up. And I dream about her. I'm underground, hiding or
dead or something, and I can't breathe. I can't push the ground
off me. I can't move. I keep looking for that guy. I even think I
see him sometimes and I get ready and it's not him. Everywhere
I go, I think he's watching me. You can't see at night. Like at the
movies, tonight. He could just come up, come up out of nowhere
again. So I got to stay ready, I got to be ready this time. I want
a gun. I think about a gun all the time. Then I'd be ready… But
I—I—can't trust myself. I'll shoot somebody else, I know I will.
I hit you, didn't I? I hit you! So a knife, I'll carry a knife—and—
and I do, all the time. I have a knife. But they don't let you have
a knife in school and I know he was there, he was watching
Sandy there, at school. He was watching all of us all over. He
called her by her name. And me. He called me by my name,
too. He was watching me, too. I wish he'd come back. I even
went out to the cemetery looking for him, calling for him, but he
wasn't there. I'm sorry I hit you. You can hit me back, I won't
do anything. I'm sorry I hit you.

Groaning Up

By Jim Chevallier

MALE, mid-teens

This is a brief monologue that may be used to satisfy a shorter audition time limit. It is an entertaining monologue that asks the ultimate philosophical question, "What's so great about growing up?" The unnamed male character has an amusing point of view and offers an ingenious response to the age-old question. There is a comic tone in the proposal, but serious elements of doubt and despair emerge in the unnamed character's tirade.

So, what's so great about growing up? The way it looks to me, everything slows down. It's like they put you in this harness and then they make you pull and the next thing you know you're an ox—big and heavy and slow. And dull. That's the worst part. You look at people over thirty and you know exactly how they're going to be. They've got their job, and they've got their ideas, and maybe they're married, and so they've got that, too. And they just get into their groove and they start walking it, you know? They just keep going round-and-round in it until it becomes this rut. And after a while, it gets so deep that the best they can do is not to sink in it. Sink until they disappear. So, what I'm saying is, what's the point? Why would you want to end up like that, when you can be young and take chances and have ideas? You know, while you can still be somebody? Have a life. Why would you want to do that, huh? Why would you want to just, like, give up? It's not like you don't have a choice.

Immortality

By David Sawn

BOY, late teens
From *A Child Went Forth* (Pioneer Drama Service)

> *The rivalry and animosity between the old and young is
> an age-old archetype. Old men struggle to hold on to their
> dwindling power, while the young, sensing weakness, rise up
> in challenge. In this scathingly blunt monologue, a frustrated
> and angry youth lashes out at an older man, mocking the
> elder's physical decline and inevitable death. He fails to
> recognize that echoes of his own curses will someday fall
> back on himself when it is eventually his turn to give way to
> the next generation. The actor is advised to avoid rushing this
> diatribe. Instead, break it up into smaller beats, insert pauses
> to breathe, and build pace and volume steadily to the climax.
> Give special weight and emphasis to the final pause, when all
> the anger is spent.*

You are very lonely and tired. You can't wait to die. It's funny,
isn't it? How we try all the time not to think about dying.
Like… it's for somebody else, right? We don't want to get old…
(Mean.) …like you, old man. But when we do get old and we
have to wake up every morning and look at the sun, it doesn't
warm us anymore. Then we want to die so quickly. But we can't.
Something won't let us, and we hang on and on and on. And we
get bitter, and we forget how to love. *(Puts a hand out, as if to
stop the old man.)* Not yet, old man! You have so many reasons
to face yourself and you can't do it, can you? Can you, old man?
Your hair is white and spare, your skin is wrinkled and dry, your
teeth are yellow and loose, your eyesight is very bad, you drool,
you can't even hear like you used to. Remember? Remember,
old man! What were you like when you were my age? Do you
remember? Do you? Your skin was alive and supple, your hair
was full and rich, your eyes sparkled and danced, you had strong
teeth, all of those things. *(Laughs.)* Every one of them like a…

a television commercial! Right? Remember? Remember what it was like to be young? *(Taunting.)* Did you think then that you would be like this one day? Did you, old man? You didn't think about it at all, did you? You didn't worry about it. It couldn't happen to you, could it? But it did! And why? Why did this happen to you, and not to someone else? Isn't that the way you planned it? You kept hoping, didn't you, old man? Maybe they would come up with a new wonder drug before it happened to you, right? Maybe you could live forever! Yes! You did! Everybody does. Everybody wants to live forever! They want to get to be maybe twenty-five or thirty, then stop! Stop growing old, stop everything and just live forever. Just like that. *(Softens.)* Why can't you love anymore, old man?

Last First Kiss

By Chad Beckim

PETER, age 18

Peter, a handsome, popular, self-confident senior in high school, has taken his girlfriend, Gabby, to the senior prom and she is later stunned to see Peter kissing another boy. Peter tries to explain what has happened, and the sobering truth that there is more that now divides them than unites them. But there is also some hope that will allow Peter and Gabby to break through this web of temporary grief and bitter feelings, and to once again reach out to each other as friends.

This isn't going to make much sense to you because this doesn't make much sense to me, but I'm going to say it because if I stop to think about it I might not ever say it. Okay? So just let me talk and then we'll deal with the aftermath. *(Takes a breath.)* When I was eight, I caught my mom stuffing my Christmas stocking. Caught her red handed, hand in the stocking, assorted trinkets in her other hand, no room for explanation. So at eight? No Santa—he's dead to me. So I know this—fact—there is no Santa. But even after that, even after I knew, I wanted so badly to believe in Santa that I, what, I tricked myself. For another three years I tricked myself. And now? We're here. But that's not all... you ready? Here goes... I love you, Gabby. I really do. When we started... dating... I kept thinking that things would, whatever, change and all that. That I would become attracted to who I am supposed to be attracted to. That didn't happen. And I'm sorry for that. But it doesn't change the fact that I love you, in spite of me, because of, because... you are the best person I know. The best. There's no denying that. You are the best. And I am sorry, Gab. You have no idea how sorry I am that this happened tonight, of all nights. I never would have planned this, you have to understand that, never in a million years, because that would make me slime. It just happened. You have to believe that. But... if there were ever going to be someone, a girl—no, a woman... it would... be you. And I don't mean that in some sort of, cereal box, consolation prize way, but in a way that's as honest as anything I can ever say. If there was? It would be you. Does that make sense?

Raising Mom

By Mike Thomas

JERRY, early 20s

Jerry, a gentle and sincere young man, has always been self-aware and shown genuine compassion for the plight of others. In this excerpt, however, he recalls an unpleasant confrontation with his mother—whom he saw shoplifting when he was a child. Although the possibility of a genuine and meaningful relationship between mother and son is highly unlikely now, Jerry still tries to reconcile himself to the sad reality of his mother's addiction and their strained relationship.

Mom used to give me these nice gifts to give to my teachers when I was in elementary school. Valentine's Day earrings, little things like that. But we never had a lot of money, and the teachers would just look at me and smile, but say, "No, thank you." I didn't want Mom to feel hurt or anything, so I just threw them away after school and told her the teachers said they were pretty. As I got older, I saw what was happening. I'd be coming around the end of the aisle in K-Mart and I'd see her putting something in her purse—a comb, or some toothpaste, or maybe a necklace. I was fourteen when a guy in a blue suit just stepped right in front of us. Mom told me to wait in the parking lot. It got so late, I didn't know if she was ever coming out of the store. Then she came out, got in the car and we drove away. I never said anything. We never shopped there again, even though it was the closest place. I used to play it over and over in my head how I'd ask her to please quit "taking things," or maybe I'd say "stealing stuff" instead. I was scared of losing her. What if she got arrested? But I never said nothing and she kept taking stuff. Then, last year I was walking out the front door to meet my friends at the bowling alley, and Mom was watching reruns. "Be careful, Jerry, I love you," and I turned around and screamed at her, "I love you, too—could you stop stealing stuff in the store!" Just like that. It just came out of me like I was barfing. She gave me this hard look like I was clear outta line. I thought she was going to deny it, but instead she said, "I didn't know it bothered you." And I said it did, it bothered me a lot, and tears just started coming out of my eyes. I told her how it scared me that she might be taken away from me and we only had each other. But she was real calm. "Well," she said, "I only take things to give other people." But she promised me she wouldn't do it anymore and went back to watching her reruns. I haven't seen her do it in a long time. But since that day, things have been different with me and my mom. In some ways I'm sorry I ever said anything. You're not supposed to have conversations like that with your mother.

Shared Interest

By Eleanor Harder

TONY, age 18
From *Rememberin' Stuff* (Pioneer Drama Service)

A teenage alcoholic downplays his addiction while recalling the nearly tragic event that brought him into rehab. Passing through layers of denial and making light of his problem, Tony eventually discloses a fundamental fault in his character that casts doubt on his chances of recovery—and survival.

Yeah, I share an interest. Share it with a lot of people. Alcohol. So, okay, what's that got to do with the price of beans? Well, 'cause I'm rememberin' stuff—rememberin' when I got busted for drunk driving. Everybody says I was lucky not to get myself killed or kill somebody else. And I know I was lucky 'cause the car was totaled. So, for awhile I got smart and quit driving when I was drinkin'. *(Grins.)* But I was still drinkin'. Y'know, man, I mean—it helps you forget your problems. Well, *(Shrugs.)* helped me, anyhow. So, like, I don't remember when I started. I just know I'd drink anything in sight that had alcohol in it, anytime I could find it. Which wasn't hard. Not at my old man's place. Hell, it was easier to find his booze than to find him. So anyhow, now I'm in one of those counseling programs. You know, for *(Makes quotation marks in the air with his fingers.)* "substance abusers." I didn't think alcohol counted as a "substance." I mean, we got potheads and speed freaks and you name it in our program. But my counselors, I don't know, they consider alcohol a substance, and me a substance abuser. Well, actually, my official title is "an alcoholic." Hey, at my age I got a title already. It's an okay program. I mean, if it can keep me from windin' up like my old man, who's a real loser, then I'm willin' to give it a try. For a while, anyhow. You know, see how it goes. I haven't had a drink this time around for three months.

Three months and sixteen days, to be exact. So, no big deal, you say, huh? Well, for an "alcoholic substance abuser" it is a big deal, lemme tell ya. *(Nods, as if to himself.)* So, okay, why did I get started drinking in the first place? I don't remember that. I mean, some things you remember, and some things you don't. Right? I've thought about it, but—well, there's this little story I really like. Says a lot, I think. See, there's these two twins, and some dude says to one of 'em, "Hey, Joe, how come you drink?" And Joe says, "'Cause my old man's an alcoholic." And then this dude asks the other twin, "Hey, Moe, how come you don't drink?" And Moe says, "'Cause my old man's an alcoholic." *(Chuckles.)* Yeah. I like that one. *(Shrugs.)* So, guess I'm the first twin, huh?

Talking to Strangers

By Martha Patterson

HARRY, early 20s
From *Talking to Strangers*

Harry, a rugged but emotionally fragile young man, continues to struggle with a profoundly disturbing relationship he had with an older woman in his mother's book club when he was still in high school. Here, he recalls the life-changing incident with compassion and ruthless self-scrutiny. But he also struggles to understand his youthful willingness to take such risks and to pay the emotional price for jumping into a relationship that had no realistic future.

My very first time? Well, it was an older woman, if you want to know the truth. She was a member of my mother's book club. This woman was a widow and she basically seduced me. She was around forty. My mother would have died if she'd known. This woman commissioned me to do a painting of her house, a watercolor. It was my first job—I was still in high school. When she hired me, I couldn't believe I'd landed my first job as an artist. And for a couple of weeks every day I'd be sitting outside, painting her house. And one day she invited me in for coffee, only it turned out to be scotch and sodas, and she just… seduced me. Right there on her velvet sofa. It was incredible. I never felt so lucky. This went on every day until I finished her painting. Then a month went by. And I had no reason anymore to go over to her house, because I'd finished the painting. So I waited. She never made an effort to get in touch. I kind of thought she would. I was waiting for it. And one day, after a month had passed, I called her. I guess I just wanted the sex. She said she was busy. I never talked to her again… my mother's book club disbanded because no one was reading the books. Funny how things work out.

Chapter 4:
Tragedy and Trauma

In this next set of monologues, the characters share their reactions to experiences that have had long-lasting, impactful, and sometimes fatal consequences. Some respond to what seems to be an uncaring world, while others try to find good, or at least meaning, in a traumatic or tragic event. They may struggle with mental illness. At least one is about an innocent who suffers simply for trying to do the right thing. Others feel a profound sense of guilt or remorse for being responsible for the destruction of another person's life, or for tearing apart important relationships.

How does a person cope with their own capacity for evil, cruelty in society, feelings of powerlessness, abandonment, self-destructive urges, or the apparent randomness of suffering? How can one make amends when a moment of ignorance or thoughtlessness causes irreversible damage to oneself and others? These are profound questions that the art of drama is uniquely qualified to pose, and the effective presentation of these monologues can have a lasting impact on the audience that goes well beyond the context of an audition.

These monologues are set in the aftermath of critical moments, so it is not necessary for the actor to fully reenact the event as if it is happening in the present. The characters have had time to reflect on what occurred, but that shouldn't diminish the emotional investment in the role. The actor should focus on determining what the character wants to relate, and why it is so important to share his experience. This will add an urgency to the presentation, which will allow the audience to vicariously relive the traumatic or tragic experience that haunts the character.

Blue

By Christopher Woods

BLUE, aged 17

Blue, a conscientious and dedicated high school student in a small rural town, recently completed training for the Volunteer Fire Department. Sensitive and well-meaning, Blue describes a perilous house fire that killed an entire family. He also offers some sobering commentary and a harrowing revelation about the cause of the fire and the haunting consequences of his actions.

I just saw Dr. Mason. Now I know. It's all too fast. Just two weeks ago, I finished training for our town's Volunteer Fire Department. That's when we got a call. My first. A house on fire. Neighbors said there were still people in there. We went in as best we could through the smoke and pulled out a family. Father, mother, two kids. Then we went to work. I got the little girl. Maybe five. Blue lips. I thought she was dead, but the Captain said to try to bring her back. Such a small thing. I laid her out on the grass. She didn't move. All limp. Like a doll. I started mouth to mouth. My first time. Her lips… so cold. So, so cold. I could see her face turning blue. I was so close to her. But I kept on, like they taught us. After twenty minutes, the Captain put his hand on my shoulder. It's okay, boy, he said. She's gone. I couldn't stop. I kept trying, mouth to mouth. Finally, the Captain and another guy pulled me away. I stood there, shaking, trying not to cry. Had I done something wrong? If I had done a better job, would that little girl still be alive? I went home that night, but couldn't sleep. In the morning the Captain called. The fire was arson. I asked him, who would burn down a house on purpose? Then the Captain said something that scared the hell out of me. He wanted me to go see Dr. Mason. I'm fine, I said. Just do it, he said. So I did. I went to see Dr. Mason. I've known him forever.

He delivered me if you want to know. That's when I learned about the fire. How the family had set it. How they were sick with that new disease. You know, the one with the long name? They knew they had it, and didn't want to spread it. So they decided to die together. How were we supposed to know? It's late now. My fever has started. I'm feeling sick. Weak. When Dr. Mason told me I had it too, he had a tear in his eye. He put his hand on my shoulder. Said he was sorry. I don't have much time left. It's crazy. All I wanted was to help. All that family wanted was to keep the disease from spreading. We all tried, didn't we? I think so. Wouldn't you have done the same thing?

Dad Left on Some Fast Reindeer

By Mike Thomas

TONY, late teens

Tony, a genuine and sincere young man with a good heart and sensitive insight, recalls with bitterness and rage his innermost secrets and fears the night his father said he had to run down to the store for cigarettes... and then never returned. At times pathetic, at other times heart-breaking, Tony is desperate for love and normality in his shattered world. This deeply affecting portrait of the changing nature of the family in our society is filled with pathos and dramatic power.

It's Christmas, okay? It's raining and it's Christmas Eve. And we're sitting around, opening gifts, drinking soda. Me, Mom, Dad, and my little brother Matt. And Dad says he's out of cigarettes and he's gonna run down to the store real quick before Santa drops by. *(Pause.)* And he never comes back. Mom didn't seem too surprised. After about two hours, Mom just sort of... started crying, rocking back and forth, crying. I hugged her tight and said I was going to bed, but I just sat in the hall. My little brother Matt asked where Daddy was and my mom told him, "Daddy left on some fast reindeer tonight." And Matt asked if he was going to come back, and Mom started singing Christmas carols. And the room glowed all weird with the Christmas tree lights blinking against the rain. I wanted to tell her that we'd all be fine without him, but I couldn't speak to my mom like that, so the next morning I broke every ashtray in the house. I broke thick, green glass ones. I broke white plastic ones. I even broke the ugly purple one I gave him on Father's Day when I was ten—hit 'em all with Dad's sledgehammer. I went through every closet and Dad's desk drawers. I broke every single ashtray in the house. I thought that would make my mom stop crying, but she got mad at all the glass in the driveway and made me clean it up. I never could talk to her right. I don't know who I am sometimes. But I know one thing. I hate Christmas.

The History of Invulnerability

By David Bar Katz

BENJAMIN, middle-aged
From *The History of Invulnerability*

> *Benjamin, a Jewish prisoner at Auschwitz during World War II, fantasizes about taking action to break out of the death camp. Here, he shares his skepticism about other prisoners who "blindly go to their deaths like sheep," believing that they are really only going to take a shower after a long journey. This sensitive and provocative character sketch is a haunting monologue that fuses moral as well as psychological themes and strips away layers of deceit and prejudice to ultimately reveal man's inhumanity to man.*

Listen to me, Joel. It's only because when they arrive here, they can't accept the truth of this place. They don't want to believe it, so they go in there hoping they're really showers. That's not weakness. To walk in there and not believe, even as they hear the guards up on the roof with the pellets, even as they breathe that gas… don't let anyone tell you that's weakness. Anyone can suspect, anyone can hate, anyone can think the worst. Some of the greatest minds in Europe have died thirty feet from where we're standing now. Do you think they were fooled by those cheap fake shower heads? By Nazi guards telling them to tie their shoes together so they can find them when they're done showering? Do you know how much strength it takes not to believe what your eyes are telling you? To not believe what men can do? I don't have such strength. To believe man can do what they do here? To conceive of this horror is to be able to do it. God bless them for not accepting what's all around them! God bless them for not believing the truth. We all cling to our own fantasies, Joel.

Just Like I Wanted

By Rebecca Schlossberg

JOEY, late teens
From *Just Like I Wanted* (Playscripts, Inc.)

> *Here is a candid snapshot of a young, rebellious boy caught at*
> *that moment between adolescence and adulthood when many*
> *young people first go out into the world armed with their*
> *own beliefs and ideas developed as teenagers. Unfortunately,*
> *however, that is not Joey's game plan. After an aggressive*
> *and violent outburst in group therapy, Joey commits suicide.*
> *Here he explains to the audience why he committed the act,*
> *as well as the unexpected results of his decision.*

For the second time in my life, I attempted suicide. And for the second time in my life, along with being Hayley's older brother, I succeeded at something. That night I used a canister of sleeping pills, twenty-seven to be exact, to kill me. Just thought you'd be curious on how I did it. When my mom found out what happened, she cried. But she always cried anyway. When my dad found out, he yelled. But he always yelled anyway. If I was aiming to change something about the way my parents acted, I didn't change a thing. But I jumped out of the burning building just the same. People'd only think about me after I was gone. That made sense to me. That was logic. After all, people only act when something happens. One thing was clear. This time, I got myself into a hole I couldn't dig my way out of. This time, all I could do was stay in. So I buried myself inside my own hole. My own coffin. Already dug. All I did was seal it up and sleep inside it. No more holes. Just sleep. Just like I wanted. I'd pictured my funeral before. Dozens of times. Over and over, actually. Like a record. Turns out, I was right. I was right about pretty much everything.

My Room

By Charles Belov

BEN, early teens

> *Ben, a young juvenile who is inwardly wracked by emotional*
> *tension and an inability to fit in with society's expectations,*
> *has been referred to Juvenile Court for psychiatric evaluation*
> *after having trashed the contents of his bedroom in a fit of*
> *rage. Here, the troubled young boy is speaking to a therapist*
> *and the impact is astonishing as the troubled teen reflects on*
> *his recent tirade. His confession calls attention to the empty*
> *promises life makes, and the way experience never prepares*
> *us for the cruel facts of life.*

Order frightens me. The thought of coming home from school, walking into my room, and having a place for everything and everything in its place, fills me with terror. My video game in the bookcase, the controls in the drawer under the TV, the bed made, no leftover pizza from three days ago... petrifying. So, a year ago, I put a lock on the door, so my mom can't get in and clean. Anyway, I get home from school yesterday, and the lock is gone and it's been replaced with a regular doorknob. Everything in that room is at right angles to everything else. Not a spot of food anywhere. I storm into the kitchen, and my mom's there, and I yell at her, "What did you do to my room?" And she's all, "We had to clean it, dear, it was drawing ants." And I start cursing and screaming, and my dad comes in with his belt off—did I tell you he believes in spanking?—and he's like, "You shut up right now and go to your room or you're going to get it." Oh, and he drinks, too. So I head back to my room, and I shut the door, and push the bed up against it so they can't open it. And I start throwing everything off my bookshelves onto the floor. Then I pick up a book and rip a page out. Then I rip another page out. A third page. Fourth. Fifth. When I get to the end of the book I pick up another one. One page. Two. Three.

And another book. I'm getting paper cuts here and there, and I don't care. Did I mention they're knocking on the door every fifteen or ten or five or two minutes? "I'm studying!" I yell. "Open the door. We want to see you," my mom says. And dad's all like, "You apologize to your mother." And mom is all, "We just want what's best for you." Meanwhile, I've started on my pile of CDs that I haven't touched in five years because it's all in the cloud and I break one. Then another. Then another. They all come apart with this satisfying snap. Video games out of their packages. Bed sheets onto the floor. Three hours. An incredibly satisfying mess everywhere. And finally, there's nothing more to destroy. And wouldn't you know, they've called the police! "Come out here, son. We just want to talk to you." That's the cop, not my parents. I'm not their son. "I'm just studying." And I look out the window, and I see my father has put a ladder up against the side of the house and he's staring into my bedroom with this look of horror in his eyes, and his face all curled up in rage. And I know that my tired arms and hands and paper cuts are a badge of honor, that I have done the right thing. And even if you put me away, I won't have to deal with my mother cleaning my room ever again.

Pictures on the Internet

By Daniel Guyton

CHRISTIAN, mid-teens
From *Pictures on the Internet* (JAC Publishing)

A teenager tries to explain why he shared an inappropriate photograph of his unsuspecting girlfriend with the world, and the tragic consequences of his actions. Although his confession is emotionally honest and powerful, it is an unforgettable story of betrayal and self-destruction. Perhaps it will awaken our conscience to an understanding that having "good intentions" is not always enough to justify betraying a friend.

I... don't know why I did it. I really liked her though, you know? But... she sent me... *(Small pause.)* I showed my friends. I thought... I must be pretty cool. I took something very personal and showed the world. I only meant to show my friends, but... they showed their friends, and they showed their friends. Even some of the teachers got it. I didn't even ask her to send it. I... We made out a couple of times. Behind the lunch room. We never even... I liked her. You know? I... told her I wanted to... you know. And she got uncomfortable. Told me she wasn't ready yet. I told her it was all right, but... she knew I was disappointed. In retrospect, I wasn't even *that* disappointed. The making out was really cool. But... my friend Eddie kept teasing me that I had not had sex yet... and I don't know. I took it out on her, I guess. When she left, I didn't even say goodbye. I just... left. Later that night, she texted me a picture. She took her shirt off, and... texted me her picture. I think she was saying she was sorry. For... disappointing me somehow. If I could do it again, I would have saved that picture. Locked it up with a password. Something special just for me. I've seen naked pictures before, but... not someone I'd ever met. Just pictures on the... Just... pictures on the internet. Nothing real. Just pixels. You know?

Eddie was over that night. When Rebecca sent the text. If he wasn't there, I... *(Small pause.)* I wish I had time to think about it, but he saw the picture almost as soon as I did. He asked me to forward it to him, and... I did. I can't believe she committed suicide over it. I just... It doesn't even seem real, you know? It's just... pixels. Random dots of color on a screen. They don't even make sense to me anymore.

Rabbit Hole

By David Lindsay-Abaire

JASON, late teens
From *Rabbit Hole* (Dramatists Play Service, Inc.)

Jason, a conscientious and sincere teenager, has written a letter to Becca and Howie Corbett to express his sorrow for the life-shattering accident that recently killed their son, Danny. The couple has now begun to drift apart and Jason hopes to point them to a path of reconciliation that will lead them back into the light of day. Although unanswered questions still linger, overtones of larger truths are revealed and deeper meanings are brought into light as Jason's letter helps the Corbetts heal.

Dear Mr. and Mrs. Corbett, I wanted to send you my condolences on the death of your son, Danny. I know it's been eight months since the accident, but I'm sure it's probably still hard for you to be reminded of that day. I think about what happened a lot, as I'm sure you do, too. I've been having some troubles at home, and at school, and a couple of people here thought it might be a good idea to write to you. I'm sorry if this letter upsets you. That's obviously not my intention. Even though I never knew Danny, I did read that article in the town paper, and was happy to learn a little bit about him. He sounds like he was a great kid. I'm sure you miss him a lot, as you said in the article. I especially liked the part where Mr. Corbett talked about Danny's robots, because when I was his age I was a big fan of robots, too. In fact I still am, in some ways—ha, ha. I've enclosed a short story that's going to be printed in my high school lit magazine. I don't know if you like science fiction or not, but I've enclosed it anyway. I was hoping to dedicate the story to Danny's memory. There aren't any robots in this one, but I think it would be the kind of story he'd like if he were my age. Would it bother you if I dedicated the story? If so, please let me know. The printer deadline for the magazine is March 31st. If you tell me before then, I can have them take it off. I know this probably doesn't make things any better, but I wanted you to know how terrible I feel about Danny. I know that no matter how hard this has been on me, I can never understand the depth of your loss. My mom has only told me that about a hundred times—ha, ha. I of course wanted to say how sorry I am that things happened the way they did, and that I wish I had driven down a different block that day. I'm sure you do, too. Anyway, that's it for now. If you'd like to let me know about the dedication, you can email me at the address above. If I don't hear from you, I'll assume it's okay. Sincerely, Jason Willette. *(Pause.)* P.S. Would it be possible to meet you in person at some point?

Real Life

By David Marquis

BILLY, mid-teens
From *Real Life* (Dramatic Publishing Co.)

> *Billy, a teenage gang member, shares a horrific and
> ultimately self-defining event from his life on the streets.
> His concise, introspective recollection of events is powerful
> and uncompromising as he describes one stunning, deeply
> disturbing, and fatal moment. This is a seething commentary
> on the nature of judgment and justice in a world where
> traditional values have declined and humanity seems bent on
> self-destruction.*

Funny thing, but your memories don't die. It was a hot summer
night. I was sitting down on the steps of my front porch with
some of my homeboys just chillin'. It was me, Terry, Robert,
and Charles. I went upstairs to get us somethin' to drink. But
when I came back down, Terry already had somethin' to drink.
'Cause he used to drink, but we didn't drink. So he was drunk
and talkin' all loud and then he pulled out a gun and he asks us,
"Who wants to play Russian Roulette?" And everybody said no,
not me—we don't fool with that. So he said he'd show us what
a real man can do. So he took out all the bullets, put one back
in. So we just went on about our business, talkin', but we were
keepin' our eye on him 'cause he was drunk. *(Snaps his fingers.)*
We heard the click. We turned around and asked him what he
was doin'. He said, "I told you what I'm doin'—showin' you
what a real man can do." But he didn't have to prove nothin' to
us 'cause he was bigger than the rest of us anyway. So we tried
to encourage him to put the gun down. We just went on talkin'
again, but still keepin' an eye on him 'cause he was drunk.
SNAP. Heard another loud click. We turned around 'cause we
knew it was getting serious then 'cause the bullet was in there
and we knew it was bound to go off sooner or later. So we tried

to encourage him more and more to put the gun down, but he didn't. Instead, he asked Robert if he wanted to play, and for some reason, Robert said yeah, he wanted to play. And that upset us—so we went on like we was ignoring him, but still watching him, and started talkin' again. POW! There it was. Robert laying out on the ground—quiverin' and shakin'—blood and brains running all out of his head. All me and Terry could do was just stand there and watch. The other ones ran. After a while one of them came back and called the police. Police got there. Robert—he had died. So after the funeral we had a little get-together. We were discussin' just simple things—fun things—but we all gotta go on with our lives...

Thank You for Flushing My Head in the Toilet
(And Other Rarely Used Expressions)
By Jonathan Dorf

BLUEBIRD STUDENT, early teens
From *Thank You for Flushing My Head in the Toilet*
(Playscripts, Inc.)

> *This is a complex psychological story of a young, apparently harmless student who stumbles upon an injured bird lying near the birdbath in his backyard. The first impression of this poignant picture is heartbreaking as the student gently lifts the fallen creature and appears poised to play Dr. Doolittle making a house call. Without warning, however, the episode takes a disturbing turn, and erupts into sudden rage and fury.*

There's a birdbath in my yard. In the back. We get robins, sparrows, pigeons. A lot of pigeons. Sometimes there's a cardinal. And squirrels. Yes, I know they're not birds, but maybe the squirrels think they are. I mean there's flying squirrels. Right? I've never seen one, but flying squirrels exist. Right? *(Pause.)* I like watching the birds. The real birds. The way they all kinda twitch their heads forward. *(Demonstrates a pecking motion.)* It's like they're talking to each other. Saying how's your day and how's the weather and would you like worms with that order? Sometimes when I'm bored, I make up what they'd say. Like this one pigeon, he's complaining about his taxes to a sparrow, and the sparrow's like, "Dude, maybe if you spent more time working and less time looking for handouts in the park..." I'm supposed to put water in the birdbath once a week. Today's my day. And the birds are there talking about the weather and their kids and there's a duck talking about how his cousin bought the farm and got served up in orange sauce last week. And the other birds are saying how sad that is and how sorry they are, only this one bird's not talking. He's not even in the bath. He's wet, like he was there, but he's not in there. He's on the ground under the bath, and he's trying to hop up. Only he can't. There's something wrong with his left wing. He can't flap it like the right one. And he's spinning around in a circle, like he's break dancing— only he's not. I go over to the bath, and they all scatter when I get close. Except for the break dancing bird. It's a bluebird—I don't remember when I've ever seen a bluebird in our backyard, and now there's one spinning like a merry-go-round under the birdbath. He's beautiful. He's flapping his right wing like crazy, but the poor little guy can't go anywhere. And he's going nuts when I pick him up in my hands. I hold him real tight so he won't scratch me, and I've got my thumb and finger around his neck to keep him from biting me. "Don't worry, little bird, I've got you." And I hold him. The phone rings in the house. I'm the only one home, but I don't move. I've got this beautiful, living thing in my hands, and that's more important than— *(Pause.)* The longer I hold him, the less he fights. He knows he's safe. I'm like the Dr. Doolittle of my backyard. And then I start to squeeze my finger and thumbs together. Around his neck. Around its neck. Tighter and tighter. The bluebird starts going crazy. I know it can't breathe, and I don't stop. I keep going—because I can. I keep going until it's—It feels good. It feels good, because for once in my life, I'm not the bird.

You Been Lied To

By Barbara Lhota and Janet B. Milstein

JACK, young adult

Jack, a compassionate and easygoing young man who resists vindictive urges, is stunned to learn from a stranger that the woman he thought was his sister is, in reality, his biological mother. Jack is quick to deny this unsettling relationship as a baseless, unfounded rumor, and a violent confrontation follows. Although unanswered questions still linger, Jack slowly sinks into a melancholy state of fading joy and disillusionment as his whole world comes slowly tumbling down around him.

Well, I'm ready to hear this explanation. 'Cause this is the most screwed up thing ever. I mean, here I am just hangin' out on my porch one day. Life's as it always is, and some dude starts telling me he went to high school with my mom. I'm thinkin' he means my sister—he's talkin' about you, not Edith—'cause he's your age. So I'm not listening all that well—thinkin' about something else. Then he says, "So how is your mom? Is she as hot as she always was?" I want to pop him in the face, but I'm totally confused at the same time. My mom's about fifty years old, so I don't think she was ever hot to him. And if she was, I want to throw up. I say, "I'm confused," and he starts laughing. I tell him that he must have things backwards because my mom's around fifty, but he tells me I'm wrong. He says he knew my mom Pam from high school. She got pregnant like eighteen years ago. She got around with a lot of guys, he says. He says her mother, Edith, was not pregnant. He notices that I look about eighteen. He laughs. "Get it?" he says. "Get what I'm sayin'?" I grabbed his shirt—suddenly, like outta nowhere. I just start poppin' him good ones. He didn't even see them comin'. He pushes me hard. And I'm layin' there. He spits and says real dramatic, "You been lied to, boy." Laughs. *(Pause.)* And I feel like my brain was just put in a blender.

Chapter 5:
Hope and Gratitude

The monologues in this section, while not necessarily light-hearted, are essentially optimistic and upbeat. The themes deal with aspiration, thankfulness, supporting others, positive role models, and the value of each person, no matter how humble.

Performing these heartfelt monologues won't require the same emotional demands as more dramatic ones in other sections, but they should still be performed with genuine feeling.

If the monologue is a tribute to an inspirational person, be sure to invest as much preparation in developing that character as the one you are playing. Make that person as real as possible in your imagination, filling in details that might not be obvious in the text. Hold the mental image of that person before you as you perform, so the audience can see you connecting to the subject of your monologue. The speaker has been shaped in some way by this other person. What qualities or values has that character taken on as a result, and why is it important to share that with the audience?

In other monologues, the focus is on a humble, underachieving, or somewhat pathetic character. He may be sharing his hopes and dreams or contemplating the meaning of life in such a way that the audience recognizes their own loneliness, inevitable disappointment, or lack of success. It's important to avoid projecting that hopelessness in the performance of the monologue. To that character, his plan or idea enriches his life with purpose and gives him the strength to carry on. Let the audience feel the sadness or sympathy *for* the character, who is unaware of his critical faults.

One monologue deals with a near-death experience and receiving a second chance. This presents an opportunity to create apprehension, then offer relief, taking the audience on an emotional roller coaster. Modulate voice and energy levels to alternatively build and release tension until the climax of the monologue.

The Art Room

By Billy Aronson

THOMAS, 30s
From *The Art Room* (Broadway Play Publishing, Inc.)

In this eloquent, enthralling, and ultimately shattering monologue, Thomas, an adult with the mind of a child, explores a dream he had with his social worker. He is honest and lucid as he recalls the princess he encountered in his dream. There is something introspective and penetrating in Thomas that suggests a sense of desperate helplessness is beginning to build. In the end, the social worker can only stand by, stunned, as Thomas ends his heart-breaking confession.

Well, I was sinking into the mud. It was sucking me down. I could hardly breathe. I was stuck there. Then down from the sky there came this sparkling bubble. And then the bubble popped and it turned right into a princess. And she was really pretty. And she had a really pretty face. And she waved her wand. And it touched my nose. And the sky got all pretty colors. And white birds flew out. And all the mud disappeared. And I was standing there. And I was looking really clean. And I could do all these things with my arms. And so she said let's get married. And we got married and I was really, really happy. So when I woke up, I drew a picture of my beautiful princess and just stared and stared. And this is really weird. I kind of knew the face, even though I never saw it before. Do you think I ever really will find someone to marry me? I would be really nice to her. All she would have to do is cook me meals two times a day or just one time and wipe my face really slowly. She wouldn't have to stay with me every minute. She could go out every night. She could gossip with her friends. I wouldn't care if she was a great big gossip. I would just want someone to be mine and that would be so nice. *(Pause.)* Why are you crying?

Bob: A Life in Five Acts

By Peter Sinn Nachtrieb

BOB, 20s
From *Bob: A Life in Five Acts* (Dramatists Play Service, Inc.)

*Bob, an incurable optimist in his twenties, truly believes
that he is destined for great things... but is currently living
in a world of make-believe at a highway rest stop. Here is
an interesting psychological portrait with a sharp sense of
paradox and a character portrait that is abrasive, funny, and
yet profane. But there is also a sad observation about life and
loneliness—and about the way fantasy and self-delusion can
shape our inner lives. The satirical character sketch reveals
what it means to live life on the edge.*

I am going to be a hero for someone. My list of great ideas is
growing longer and stronger every day. So much I can do and
this is where it begins, Bob's diary. I can make this the greatest
rest stop in the country. I'll clean the bathrooms every other
hour. I'll carve better trails into the hills and tidy the bushes
where the men meet their soul mates. Late at night, using paint
left by the trash, I will reconfigure the parking design to foster a
greater sense of community amongst the travelers. Bob, rest stop
maverick. The Bob Memorial Rest Stop. Put it on a plaque. Do
you think when someone reads your name on a plaque hundreds
of years after you're dead, for a brief instant, you exist again?
All of a sudden the patch of mushrooms, the bit of that tree, that
soil or dust that were once your molecules suddenly experience
a moment of connectedness, a memory of their past teamwork
as being part of a human being that did something that was so
important it had to be recognized. On a plaque.

Grandpa

By Steven Bergman

TEENAGER, mid- to late-teens

A teenager faces a deeply disturbing family moment—leaving for a weekend to go to his grandfather's funeral. It is a moment never to be forgotten for those who have to witness the death of a beloved family member—and there is a profound sense of guilt and compassion in this exploration of loss that is touching. Addressing his youthful demons, the teenager confronts his burning emotions and presents a compelling argument that family is sacred and traditional values are an essential ingredient in the healing process.

It's just a weekend, I know. Two days. I'll go there, see everyone, pay my last respects to the old man, and come back. No sweat. Aw, who am I kidding? I'm gonna really miss Grandpa. He was ornery all right. I'll give him that, but he always stuck to his convictions. He was my family's equivalent to that guy Archie Bunker. You know, from that television show that you see on Nick at Nite all the time? I remember once, when I was a little kid, how he made me cry hysterically. How? Well, I was six years old and he took me bowling. Now, when you take a little kid bowling, aren't you supposed to just let the kid do their thing—even if they bowl gutters the entire afternoon? Not Grandpa. He was determined to make me into the next champion of the Professional Bowlers Association. At six! So, no matter how many pins I managed to knock down, he would tell me how to fix it for the next frame. "Move left, move right, keep your arm straight!" I never did it right, so there was always something he corrected me on, until finally I was so frustrated that I burst into tears because I wanted to stop. He didn't understand. There I was, crying at the bowling alley because I had enough, and Grandpa couldn't understand why. Now I know that he was just trying to help, but back then I was just a kid being yelled at by a grownup. *(Pause.)* I also want to be there for my mom. You only lose your father once in life, and they were very close. Grandpa never wanted her to marry my father, but when it comes right down to it, Grandpa went along with it for almost forty years. I also notice a lot of Grandpa in me today. I'm not saying that I'm gonna go around yelling at six-year-olds all the time, but I hope that I'll be as true to my convictions as Grandpa was. I'm gonna miss him a lot. I love you, Grandpa.

God in Bed

By Glenn Alterman

STEVEN, early 20s

Here is a thought-provoking and engrossing monologue that explores what it feels like to almost die. Steven, a young man with a care-free attitude, finds himself in the middle of a skidding car accident, spinning round and round. He has to confront two starkly different realities—life and death—finally tapping into the essence of what it truly feels like to be human, and discovering the self-awareness and compassion for others that comes when the truth of one's fragile life is revealed.

My hands, like this, clutched on the wheel. But the car kept swerving out of control! I tried turning, but nothing! And all I could think was, "Why me? Why now?" as the car kept skidding, turning. And the other cars passing, honking at me. Beeping, like I'm doing it on purpose, right? And your life, your life flashes by. Just like they say. From your first memory on, bing-bing-bing! And I sat there, helpless. My God, it was like watching a movie. But me, *I* was the movie! And my car had a life of its own, spinning round and round in circles. And me, a piece of putty, strapped in my seat belt. Beyond terror—beyond beyond! Ready to die, cash in the chips. My death imminent! But then, the strangest thing happened. Wait, wait'll you hear this! I'm sitting there, right? Preparing to die. The car going round in circles. When for absolutely no reason at all—the car stopped! I kid you not. And I found myself comfortably parked by the side of the road, inside a giant snowdrift. Encased, like in a white cocoon. Everything still and quiet, except for the windshield wipers going back and forth, back and forth. And the snow falling. And of course my heartbeat pounding all over the front seat. There I was on this quiet night, sitting in the front seat of my car, *not dead*. No, not even a scratch. Nothing. Just sitting there with my mouth wide open like this. *(Demonstrates.)* But then... then I made this sound. Like a whimper, like a little whimper. Like a baby in a crib. And the sound opened up, more and more, more and more! Until I was crying, wailing! Tears pouring down my face. But then something inside me whispered, "It's okay, it's okay. It's over and you're not dead." And I said, "Thank you. Thank you, God! Thank you! Thank you!" And I stopped crying. And you know what I did? Know what I did then? I started to laugh! Laugh, laugh, laugh like a lunatic! Like a crazy man. But alive, very alive! Just sitting there in the front seat of my car. Inside of this big white cocoon, strapped in my seat belt, looking out the window at the snow... the snow... the snow. *(Gently.)* Hello, snow.

Moonboy

By Aoise Stratford

MOONBOY, age 17
From *Oracle*

*Moonboy is an astronomy geek who lives in an abandoned
apartment building and spends most of his time gazing out
at the world through his battered telescope. Weakened by
insecurity and self-doubt, Moonboy desperately searches for
some meaning in life to break the chain of his bad luck and
misfortune. In this excerpt, he tries to make friends with a
young woman he thinks is a kindred spirit, and come to terms
with the harsh reality that good luck and good fortune may be
of our own making, not an accident of fate.*

You want to know if I'm lonely? Why? Because you don't see
any other intelligent life hanging out with me, day in, day out,
on this shabby landing in this derelict apartment building? I
mean, yeah, maybe I can see why you'd think that, why you'd
say I'm a weirdo. Maybe most seventeen-year-old guys are out
doing something else. In packs, like dogs. But that's a narrow
view of the universe, don't you think? Widen your field of view
and you'll see I'm meant to be right here, in front of this broken
window with this telescope. And I am anything but alone. Once
upon a time there were dinosaurs roaming the earth. During
the day they hunted each other, hid in swamps, and lumbered
through thick undergrowth in opaque jungles where nothing
else lived. No birds called. Not yet. At night, they would graze
and search for water. The smaller ones would find crevices or
vegetation to sleep in. Did dinosaurs lie down to sleep? Not the
big ones, surely. How would they get back up? They probably
just slept like horses, standing, one eye at the ready, just in case.
As they dozed beneath the night sky, pulsing with the glow of
volcanic ash, somewhere, far off in the universe, a star was
born. They couldn't see it then, this star, because it was billions

of light years away. And because the sky was hazy, and plus they had their eyes closed, right? But—and this is the really cool thing—I can see it. We can see it. The dinosaurs are long dead, but the light that left home when they were sleeping is just reaching Earth now. That twinkle of light has been traveling for billions of years. The star it came from exploded and fizzled out who knows when, but still the light comes toward us. So when we look at the night sky, we can see stars that aren't even stars any more. It's like looking at ghosts. We are not alone. We're looking right back in time through the barrel of my telescope, back to a map of the universe that belonged to the dinosaurs. So, if we can see the past, if we can look back in time, if we could figure out how to turn the telescope around... what would we see? I know, I know, you'd see death, I suppose. Nothingness. But I say we look harder. And when we do... Yesterday, I saw a shooting star. Where was it headed? Not into the past, that's for sure. We're on a fault line, you know, and the earth buckles at a fault line just enough to vary the angle at which light hits the earth's surface. That variance, if I've calculated it correctly, corresponds to a shift in the angle of the sun that comes up every four thousand years, give or take, thanks to the earth's orbit being pulled slightly off course by the elliptical passage of Pluto. And I know that to you that sounds nuts. But nuts in comparison to what? The earth being round? The fact that relative to the cosmic microwave background you and I might look like we're just standing still, but are in fact currently moving at a speed of approximately three hundred and sixty-nine kilometers per second? Which, in case you're wondering, works out to be about two million miles an hour. So yeah, it sounds nuts. Except I'm not. And you know it. You do, I can tell. The planet is crowded with people who think we're freaks, who think there's no new way to see things, that seeing outside of time is impossible, that people who wonder what reality might become have lost touch with what reality is now—as if we can even say what now is—

and they should be locked up, no key, three squares a day. But you and I? Like I said. Kindred spirits. We're not out there with the pack, are we? At least for now, you're here, with me. We know the power of the stars. And how could any of us be lonely in a universe like that?

My Brother Adam

By Amanda Kozik

JON, mid-teens

> *In this touching character portrait, Jon celebrates and honors his older autistic brother, Adam, who is soon to graduate from high school. Although Jon's speech initially focuses on the estranged love/hate relationship he had with his brother, the tribute is still warm and comforting. He is tough-talking, sometimes hard and abrasive, until he slowly comes to the realization that his brother is a loving, witty, and compassionate sibling. Absorbing and touching, this is a heart-warming tribute to friendship and forgiveness.*

It's odd, even though my brother Adam is two years older than me, I've always thought of him as my little brother. I feel guilty for admitting it, but having a brother like Adam can be frustrating. Like any sibling, living with him isn't always easy. He can talk your ear off and he hogs the TV. What makes Adam different from other brothers is the difficulty he has understanding other people's feelings. It doesn't mean he doesn't care, though. You see, Adam's autistic. It wasn't apparent right away. Adam just seemed a little shier than other kids. We used to be close when we were little. We'd run around the backyard in the summertime, dancing in the sprinklers, and when we finally came in the house, we'd be covered in mud. When Adam cares about something, he cares about it with his whole heart. When he was eight, he was fascinated with insects, and he learned the names of all the bugs. Now, he's obsessed with baseball, as in "knows the batting average of every MLB player" obsessed. Adam was my first friend, but as we got older, we drifted apart. I was on the honor roll. As for Adam? He didn't do well in school. He was always in trouble, and he fell behind the other kids. "Behavior disorder." That was what the teachers summed it up to. Autism isn't an easy thing to diagnose, and a much harder thing to understand. They thought Adam was misbehaving. One of my friends couldn't play at my house because his mom thought my brother was a bad influence. The teachers and the other kids didn't understand that Adam's mind just worked differently, that he didn't talk and act like other kids. They couldn't comprehend the challenges Adam faced each and every day, and the things they took for granted. Growing up with an autistic sibling influences your mannerisms, the way you read people, and the way you see the world. When you're little, you don't think of their behavior or their way of talking as odd, especially not when they're older than you. With autism, simple changes and environments can be unbearable for a person, and when someone in your family is autistic, you learn to anticipate that person's reaction. I suppose I wasn't aware of it, but Adam changed my life for the better. Having Adam for a brother, I learned to read people. In his own way, he helped me develop empathy. He taught me to see the world from another point of view. I used to count the days until Adam would graduate and I'd be spared the embarrassment at school. Today, Adam is graduating. For me, high school is just a small step before college, and graduating is no big deal. For Adam, this is a huge accomplishment, one that brings him so much pride. As I see him, walking up to claim his diploma, I think of all the roadblocks he's encountered and all the hurdles he overcame. I took for granted my grades, and never thought about how hard it is for students like Adam to succeed with disabilities. The joy on his face today reminds me that I still have a lot to learn from him. I've never been prouder to call Adam my brother.

The Messenger

By Eric Bobosian

MESSENGER, undetermined age

In this complex and haunting monologue, a mysterious messenger explores the fascinating world between make-believe and reality with sensitive insight that revolves around potential madness and fantasy. It's difficult at times to be sure where the character's monologue stops and real life takes over. "The Messenger" has a sharp sense of paradox and is unrelenting and uncompromising to the last word. Although in the end unanswered questions linger, overtones of larger truths are revealed and deeper meanings surface at last.

Excuse me, you look confused. Do you know that there's a path out of your confusion? There is. It's your ego that causes your confusion. You are not the center of the universe. You are not God. You have to realize that you are nothing. Just as I have accepted that I'm nothing. I finally realized that I am nothing more than an ant crawling on a leaf on a vine in the middle of the Amazon jungle. I am one pebble on the beach. But even though I am nothing, I am part of a bigger plan. And so are you. See, like you, I used to get confused. I'd watch TV and I'd see all those rich famous people and I'd think to myself, "Why do they have everything and I have nothing?" I'd get angry. But maybe those people are being rewarded for being good? If I look at them I can see they have such nice smiles, such nice teeth. They are so beautiful, so good. No wonder good things are happening for them. They deserve it. You see, God gives you what you deserve. I'll be walking down the street and I'll see a person lying on the ground, in pain, and I'll think to myself, "Why is that person in pain? Why is that person suffering?" But I don't know why God put that person in my path. Maybe God is trying to teach me something? Or maybe that person did something? Maybe that person is a murderer? I don't know.

Maybe, probably, he did something. Otherwise, why is God making that person suffer? You know there's a lot of terrible things that happen to people in the world. A lot of things we can't understand. But that's the way it has to be. If everybody just did what they wanted all the time and had it easy all the time and nothing bad ever happened, we'd just be like a bunch of children having fun, and that wouldn't be any good, would it? So don't be confused. And don't worry. Because you are part of a bigger plan. You can't understand it and you can't change it. Have a nice day.

Rat King

By Troy Diana and James Valletti

BROOKLYN GUY, young adult
From *Tales from the Tunnel*

> *Brooklyn Guy is the devoted son of a former long-time New York City Metropolitan Transportation Authority (MTA) railroad worker who loved to hunt and kill rats. His personal story is an enthralling celebration of rat infestation and extermination filled with deadpan humor, social and political skewering, and a hefty dose of toxic satire. It is a quite mad scenario of big city culture that offers stark insight into the complex social issues faced in major metropolitan cities these days.*

My father worked for the MTA for twenty-seven years. He was always working on the tracks in some job or another, and he loved it. He'd come home with dirt all over him, singing his favorite song, "I've Been Working on the Railroad," and tell me all the stories from his days and nights on the track. My favorites were his tales of the rats. You see, when he was promoted to a Track Foreman he was in charge of a group of guys whose main purpose was, basically, to kill rats. He LOVED to kill rats. He would order his poison from his superiors—"Vengeance," they called it on the streets—and he'd smear peanut butter all over them. "The rats loved peanut butter," he told me, "and I always spiked it up!" Then the guys would go out on the tracks and look for rat droppings—the more crap on the floor, the more rodents nearby. One time, while scouting, a rat ran onto his shoe and up the right leg of his pants... *(Shudders at the thought.)* ...and came back down on the left. That's when he started tucking his pants into his boots. Smart guy! My dad got so good at his job that he started getting noticed by the media. He was affectionately dubbed the "Rat King" and he was all over the news—not only here but in England and Japan, too. I am so proud of him. My Dad, The Rat King!

The Wastes of Time

By Duncan Pflaster

JESSE, 20s
From *The Wastes of Time*

Jesse, a young man on the threshold of personal self-discovery, has formed an inexorable bond with his sensitive uncle and offers this tender narrative of regret and loss after his uncle's death. His sorrow transcends childhood memories and emotional cleansing to reach a heightened state of admiration and respect for his beloved Uncle Peter. Here, he gives way to his true feelings in a rush of unbridled passion, in what seems like a benediction. It is an epithet ripe with majestic feeling that somehow comes from hearing heart-felt words made flesh and blood.

I haven't always been iffy on religion. As a child, I was quite devout. When I was five years old, I could recite the names of all the books of the Bible in order. What use that served was beyond me, but I was rewarded for my achievements in Sunday School with extra grape juice and vanilla cookies shaped like lambs. But then, when I was about five or six, the church found out that Uncle Peter—not my real uncle, but a really close friend of my mom's—had AIDS, and they asked him not to come to their church anymore. He'd been active with the choir and stuff, and it was sort of an open secret that he was gay. A secret at church of course—we all knew—but once he had AIDS, that was just too much for the church. So, of course, my family didn't go back, either, in a show of solidarity. That was more my mom's doing—my dad just went along, since he didn't much care for going to church in any case. I asked my parents about it at the time and they told me not to ask silly questions. One day, Uncle Peter took me to the zoo—this was around the time my parents were talking about getting divorced and stuff, though they didn't want me to know, so I was spending a lot of time with Peter so they could have time alone together. And we talked a lot. He was one adult who always talked to me like I was a person. He always said I could ask him anything. He was the only one who didn't laugh when I told him I wanted to be a writer. My father said I should look for another job to make real money, since writers didn't make much. And I guess he was right, since I am a temp on the side. So, anyway, I was at the zoo with Uncle Peter and we were sitting on a park bench, and I asked him about the church kicking him out. He said that he was angry at first, but he'd decided to let it go. Then he took a deep breath, and he looked at me and said, "Jesse, don't ever let anyone tell you what you are. Always know that you are beautiful. No matter what you want to do with your life, the people who stand by you and love you anyway are your real friends and your real family. Always remember that. Remember that everything you do is a part of who you are, and you're beautiful because of that." I was a little confused—that was a lot of heavy stuff to lay on a little kid. Uncle Peter shook his head and said, "Never mind," and we went and looked at the penguins. It was this dark, damp room made to look like a cave, with a window that looked out into the lake where the penguins would swim through the water. It looked like they were flying, soaring like dark chubby angels. There, in the cave, lit only by the eerie penguin light, he looked so sad. I took this big man's hand in mine and said, "I'll remember, Uncle Peter. You're beautiful, too." He smiled suddenly and tousled my hair. He died just a year later. Eventually I grew up and lost my faith in the church, and knew I was gay, and really understood what Uncle Peter was trying to tell me. Looking back, it still seems strangely holy to me, more than anything I got from the church—it seems like a benediction, a blessing.

Chapter 6:
Outsiders

People have a tendency to think of outsiders as oddballs who don't fit into the mainstream, and there's some truth to that assertion. In these monologues, however, the individuals have typically defined themselves as not being a part of the majority *before* it is confirmed by society.

As outsiders, these characters offer a unique and personal perspective on the world to which they feel they don't belong. Some are prophets, warning of a corrupt, apathetic, dangerous, or misguided culture. Others are outlaws who reject the status quo and refuse to play the game. Several wish they could fit in, but don't know how to belong. In every case, these characters are exposed, and it is this exposure mixed with isolation that causes them emotional distress and a burning desire to communicate their point of view. All are in pain, acutely feeling their separation from the rest of humanity.

Most of these monologues focus on divisions and differences that exist between races, but there are also pieces about the persecution of political prisoners, displaced warriors, generation gaps, homelessness, and the homosexual experience. One is a chameleon outsider, a parasitic person because he has no real personality of his own.

When presenting one of these monologues, allow the character to struggle to assert his value. He will either resist powerlessness, succumb to pressures to conform, or self-destruct. Seek to persuade the listener to at least understand, if not accept, the character's perspective.

Advice to the Players

By Bruce Bonafede

ROBERT, 20s

From *Advice to the Players* (Samuel French, Inc.)

> *Robert, a Black African actor, spent a number of years in prison—most of them in solitary confinement—in protest against segregation policies of his country. In the midst of horrific conditions, he finds a way to assert some measure of control over his jailers, through passive resistance. This enthralling monologue about asserting one's humanity in an insane, inhumane world is an honest, uncompromising moment of unforgettable drama.*

You know, in my last year in prison I was most of the time alone. But once, for a while, I had a man with me. I never knew who he was. He couldn't tell me his name because when they first threw him into my cell his jaw was already so badly broken he couldn't speak. And it never healed. They made sure they beat him often enough so it wouldn't. One night they brought him back, and I listened to him die. It took hours. *(Pause.)* When they came for him again, I dared them to take me instead. They were happy to oblige. Anyway, I kept them from finding out for a few days. I even dragged his body around the cell so when they looked in they'd think he was moving. But then he started to smell, and... *(Shrugs.)* They thought I'd gone crazy when I refused to give him up. They stood in the door with their guns on me, cursing and shouting their lungs out... faces all red. I pulled him with me back against the wall, and I waited for them to shoot. *(Pause.)* And nothing happened. *(Laughs.)* I started to laugh at them standing there, watching me holding this dead man in my arms. The thing was... they were waiting, waiting for *me*, waiting to see what *I* would do. I still had choices. I could come to my senses, be a good Kaffir, and say "Ja... baas," and give him up. Or I could hold on to him until they came in and beat me. Or... I could walk straight into their guns. I could make them be the monsters they were threatening to be. Whatever happened would be because of the choice *I* made. Whatever they did would be in reaction to me. They were as bound by me as I by them because we were men in confrontation. I was still a human being, and that was something all their laws and prisons and guns and power could not take away. Could never take away. And I knew this was something our people needed to see. Something that would help them live, whether they got this... *freedom* they wanted or not.

Blacktop Sky

By Christina Anderson

KLASS, aged 27
From *Blacktop Sky*

> *Klass is a homeless young African-American man who
> lives on a bench in a run-down housing project. He has
> ceremoniously arranged various objects around him and
> now addresses them in a performance style reminiscent
> of a Baptist minister at a tent revival or Robert Preston's
> "Trouble" from The Music Man. By turns bombastic and
> prophetic, Klass offers a harrowing—and ultimately heart-
> breaking—character portrait of ravaged, tormented souls,
> and shares his tough-love blueprint to save them.*

You may not be fully aware of the times we're livin' in. The
times that they don't print in our papers or splash across our
screens or pump through our radios. I suggest you might not
be aware because I see you. I watch you. I see you holding on
to what little sanity and security you have left, squeezing it so
tight that the color is leaving your fingers, draining from your
hands. The squeezing is causing your muscles to ache. Jaws to
clench. And you think that pain is a sign of sanity? Security?
It's not, my friends. It's not. *(Pause.)* There's a wind blowin'
through you. A violent gust of truth. It starts out as a breeze
somewhere in here… *(Points at his heart.)* …and it wakes up
all the noise inside of you. Then that breeze gets in your blood.
Travels through every vein. Head to toe. It gathers enough
speed to the point where it won't let you sleep at night. That
breeze becomes a gust and that gust won't let you be still. Won't
keep your troubles quiet. You sit on stoops, lean against cars,
stand under the moon—restless. You walk to one end of your
neighborhood then back to the other end, go sit back on that
same stoop, sit under the sun—restless. The gust is stirring your
soul. It's pulling up memories from way down deep, from the

cracks and crevices covered with scabs and scars. We swallow what we think is liquor, inhale what we think is weed, inject what we think is freedom. We alter our state of reality so we don't have to participate in it. So we can't be responsible, aware, dependable. And what happens when we hear a scream? When we see someone who looks like us, cornered? Pleading? Hm? *(Turns away as if he's ignoring a weeping soul.)* We cross the street. We turn the music up a little louder. We drink, smoke, squeeze—but we still hear it. It never goes away. The wind, the noise, that somebody pleading—it's not going away. And then the next somebody is cornered. *(Turns away.)* And then the next one... *(Turns away.)* And then the next—until it's you. And then you want to know why no one's coming to save you, to take you to a safe place?

Dream of a Deer at Dusk

By Adam Kraar

JED, aged 17
From *Dream of a Deer at Dusk*

*Jed tries to impress Manoah, an innocent fifteen-year-old
girl, with a puzzling chapter of the town's history before it
figuratively became a graveyard for teenagers. Standing in
the woods next to the remains of an old, abandoned Impala
with no wheels, no hood, and a small tree growing out of the
trunk of the car, Jed weaves a dreadful story that highlights
the loss of innocence and the search for personal dignity and
relevance in a small town that has sadly eroded over time.*

This town was like a jewel. The factories—and the opera house—
and the railroad—running full blast. Now, it's like a graveyard,
with people smiling and nodding like zombies. *(Anticipates her
interruption.)* You don't know what it used to be. The streets
were like perfectly paved. There was a freakin' zoo! Now, it's just
cages, and a smell. *(Pause.)* So this kid couldn't take it anymore.
The silence of the zombies. So he hot-wires this car downtown,
peels out, waking the dead. Turns out, it's the mayor's Impala,
which His Honor had souped up so he could speed off to other
counties and drink on Sundays. Right away, the cops and the
Highway Patrol give chase. He turns into the back alleys, trying
to get out of town—if he can get to the Interstate, he's free. But
they're cutting off every artery. Highway Patrol brings out the
shotguns. Every time he tries to get on Route One, they got a
man with a 12-gauge. So finally this kid says, "Forget this!" He
charges out of Peapod Alley, onto Main Street and they open
fire. He ducks, sidewinding, eighty, ninety miles an hour. By
now, he's got two flats, black smoke pouring out of the hood.
No way he can get past these guys—it's suicide! But instead,
he takes a mad right to Walnut. Heads straight out to the woods,
drives off the road, tears up the ground, taking chunks outta

trees and doesn't stop till his motor explodes—right here. It's night now, and the whole woods light up like a nuclear fireball, brighter than day. When the cops get here, they figure he's burnt up. But they never found a body.

Good Mourning, America

By Lucy Wang

ASIAN-AMERICAN MALE, mid-20s
From *Good Mourning, America* (Original Works Publishing)

> *In this poignant and politically charged monologue, a young Asian American faces the reality of the infamous 2001 terrorist attack on 9/11 in New York City and wonders what might have happened if any of the terrorists had been Asian American. Posing uneasy questions about betrayal and prejudice, the author explores the nature of ethnic and racial contempt, jealousy, and resentment that sometimes bubbles just beneath the surface of intercultural relationships. The monologue also calls attention to our country's somewhat ambiguous attitude toward patriotism.*

My grandfather used to say there's no such thing as a bad orange in California. Of course, he used to say that as he tried to sell you a whole crate full of oranges. All kinds of oranges. Blood oranges. Valencias. Clementines. You can never have too much Vitamin C. You don't want to catch scurvy, do you? Scurvy. That was his favorite word. He used to cackle just saying it. Scurvy. Grandpa thought it was such a funny sounding word for something that means bleeding under the skin, bleeding gums. But scurvy ceased to be a barrel of laughs when the Japanese bombed Pearl Harbor. Suddenly my grandparents were considered high security risks and were taken away to internment camps. They lost their citrus orchard. They lost their sense of humor, their power of speech. So when the second plane hit, I grabbed my address book and pulled out a road map. I panicked. Where the heck am I going to go if the terrorists are Asian? Who will have the guts to protect me from illegal, immoral seizures? Do I know anyone with that kind of courage? I'm not sure I do, so I prayed to God. Please, please, dear God, don't let the terrorists be Chinese, Japanese, Korean, Filipino, Vietnamese,

Polynesian—anybody that remotely looks like me. Am I terribly ashamed that I jumped for joy when I learned the terrorists were Muslim? You betcha. Ideally, it shouldn't matter. Ideally we're, above all, Americans. Ideally, it's innocent until proven guilty. Ideally, there are no bad oranges anywhere. Grandpa, you were definitely right about one thing. You can still die of scurvy. Scurvy also means worthless, mean, contemptible. Grandpa died at Manzanar, a victim of mean, worthless contempt.

Matthew

By Sofia Dubrawsky

MATTHEW, late teens

> *Matthew, a sensitive teenager struggling to understand his sexuality, takes an unflinching look at life after one of his best friends commits suicide. This is a personal tragedy and Matthew's emotional problems are not easily disentangled. They are made more poignant, however, by his willingness to finally confront the issue, face the truth, and accept the consequences. This probing and compassionate self-portrait of the young lost souls of the world is honest and haunting.*

When I heard about Tyler Clementi jumping off the George Washington Bridge, I had this hot and cold feeling all over my body, like rivers of fire and rivers of ice, racing up and down my arms and legs. I had just got home from swim practice and I was unpacking my bag and I sunk onto the floor. My palms were all sweaty. It was like my body telling me, "Here's another chance to tell my parents." I could hear their voices, talking in the kitchen, all muffled compared to the radio blasting the news from the living room. Tyler Clementi—a young gay man, a promising music scholar, commits suicide. Can you imagine your roommate videotaping you kissing your boyfriend and streaming it live on the Internet? A few days later, he's jumping off the George Washington Bridge! *(Pause.)* Sometimes I think I could do it. I think I could. It'd be different though, like leaning in on the train just when it pulls up into 14th Street, when it's moving so fast and you feel that dirty tunnel wind pressing onto your face and then—bam! I'd just be gone. Problem solved, instantly. Wouldn't have to tell my parents then, would I? I heard that Tyler's parents knew he was gay, and they were fine with it, but that wasn't enough, was it? Look what he did. Look what he felt he had to do. What if I tell my parents and it's still not enough? Sometimes I think it will all be fine, like in a movie, maybe they already know. But then I think, what if they have no idea? What if they don't accept it, like so many other people? What will happen to me then?

My Superpower
By Lucy Wang

STAN LEE, aged 15

Stan Lee, a fifteen-year-old Asian-American firebrand, has learned over time how to protect himself and his dreams against a tide of expectations and preconceived notions. Although he can question his own existence quite forcibly, Stan Lee is often sentimental and is primarily focused now on finding his own superpowers. Here, he recalls his human strengths and weaknesses, and his well-rounded regime of preparing to become a superhero. Without realizing it, the well-ordered examination of his world is more idealistic than realistic.

When you look like me, people automatically assume that I am a… *(Gets into a stance, hands up, right leg up in the air.)* …Kung-Fu master! *(Kicks an imaginary opponent.)* Hi-yah! Take that, weak earthling… *(Left jab followed by a right cross)* …and that I have superpowers. I can kickbox, karate chop and mix martial arts you into a zillion pieces—all with my eyes closed. Not. But no one ever believes me. Never. The other boys are always trying to pick fights, challenge me. Pushing and shoving. Breaking into my locker. "Show me what you got, Stan!" I suppose it's only natural. Bruce Lee. Jet Li. *(Refers to himself.)* Stan Lee. Yeah, my parents named me after *that* Stan Lee. The guy who created Spider-Man, the Hulk and Captain America. What a terrible mistake. What were my parents thinking, giving me a name like that? You can't name a kid Stan Lee and expect him to succeed on his own without a mask, without a sword! Yes, a sword. Like this. *(Wields an imaginary épée and starts thrusting, flexing the wrist, lunging and showing off various self-defense techniques throughout the remainder of the monologue.)* It's called an épée. You grip it like a small bird in your hand. But it's no small bird. Oh, no.

Sharp. Dangerous. Quick. I could cut you if you come too close. Ask me to spin a web. Turn green. Blind you with my shield. And I could, so don't test me. My parents told me I had three career choices. Doctor. Physician. M.D. To that I say, please! Don't fence me in! Don't make me draw blood. I want to be a musician. Rock Star Performer. Write music and play the guitar. For millions and millions of adoring fans worldwide. So please, don't stand in my spotlight. I'm still exploring my powers, so if I were you, I'd keep a proper distance. *(Lunges and thrusts.)* It's for your protection and mine. Of course it's a huge risk. I could go down in flames, but superheroes risk their lives all the time. Usually for damsels in distress, furry pets and crying babies, I know. But don't you think that a superhero has to learn how to save himself before he can save others? *(Pause.)* Hello, I'm Stan Lee, and I'm working on my superpowers.

Name Me

By Rhea MacCallum

BOY, aged 14

Here is a daring, thoughtful, and provocative story that features a bittersweet and mysterious character portrait of a boy exploring some of the events that have helped shape his identity and influence his destiny. There is a good blend of humor and tenderness to help sketch a three-dimensional portrait of the character and this special moment in his life. This insightful piece also reflects something striking about embracing adventures and avoiding routines that strangle the spirit.

The little black girl with the nappy hair and dingy dress baited me again. Today she stood at the back door and beckoned me from the other side of the screen door to follow her. So I did. As I chased her through the grassy meadows sprawled between my grandmother's farmhouse and the woods, I wondered why she has chosen to haunt me. She wants to pull me into something, but what? She wants me to see her, to follow her, to know her perhaps—but she never allows me to touch her. We never get that close. When my advancement becomes too dangerous for her, she sprints off with the energy of a thousand gusts of wind, vanishing before my muscles even receive the message from my brain to move. Today, her naked feet move steadily and swiftly, even though she habitually looks back to verify that I am still following at a safe distance. During this exercise, it occurs to me that this beautiful little girl was born into a paranoia I have never known. So I fight my curiosity and keep my distance. When we arrived at the edge of the woods, where grass recedes like an aging man's hairline, I realize where she is taking me, and I prepare to follow her. Through the woods we dash together, and yet apart, making our way to the other side, where a grassy knoll covered in headstones awaits us. As we neared the end of the patch of woods, I lost sight of the little girl. Confident I know where she is leading me, I continued to charge ahead. The trees dispersed and the heavens exposed me to the blinding bright light of the noonday sun. In the shock of my exposure, I tripped over a rotting log and sliced my knee open on the way down, meeting the earth with a great thud, which echoed in the stillness of the woods. I writhed in pain, clutching my knee to my chest. Then a calm came over me, and the little girl returned. This time she came up to my side. She seemed terrified by my blood. This wasn't supposed to happen. She's so close, the closest she's ever been. I think I could reach out in a flash and have a hold on her. But that would be a violation. And she's so quick, there is no guarantee that I would actually catch her. Standing over me, waiting patiently for my strength to return to my legs, she appeared as an angel, with a brilliant halo highlighting her undone hair. I closed my eyes again and when I reopened them, she was gone. And so was the pain. So I stood and stumbled toward my destination. The family cemetery. It doesn't look anything like I remember it. Weeds and grass have grown wild and high. The little fence that surrounds the dozen or so graves has fallen in on itself. But the headstones are still visible. And there among them, a site marked only by a simple cross. Then a whisper passes through me with the sigh of the wind… "Name me." And I know why she's led me here.

Please Hear What I'm Not Saying

By Anonymous

UNSPECIFIED

> *Here is a brief audition companion piece which may be useful*
> *to satisfy a shorter one- or two-minute audition time limit or*
> *a second short audition monologue. Written as a diary entry,*
> *the piece uses the image of a mask to remind us that disguise*
> *is simply a recognition of our urgent need to reclaim a sense*
> *of personal, individual identity. The anonymous piece also*
> *illuminates the unspoken doubts about self-identity and asks*
> *penetrating questions in a language that is simple but does*
> *not provide easy or convenient answers.*

Don't be fooled by me.
Don't be fooled by the face I wear.
For I wear a mask. I wear a thousand masks.
Masks that I'm afraid to take off.
And none of them are me.
I give the impression that I'm secure,
That all is sunny and unruffled with me,
Within as well as without.
But don't believe me, please?
I'm afraid that deep down I'm nothing,
That I'm just no good, and that you
Will see this and reject me.
So I play my game, my desperate
Pretending game. With a façade of
Assurance without, and a trembling
Child within. And so begins the
Parade of masks, the glittering
But empty parade of masks.
Who am I, you may wonder?
I am someone you know very well.
For I am every man you meet, and
I am every woman you meet.

Sex, Drugs, Rock & Roll

By Eric Bogosian

HOMELESS MAN, 30s
PROPERTIES: empty paper cup

A homeless man hobbles in holding an empty paper cup. He slowly approaches, begging to one or two audience members while holding out his cup. It becomes increasingly evident that the man is a lost soul and what follows is a touching monologue about lonely—perhaps even psychotic—street people whose lives have been shaped by fantasies and frustrated dreams. Lonely and disturbed, the homeless man's sad observations about life shape not only our own lives but also the lives of those we encounter—which makes their parting all the more poignant.

Good afternoon, ladies and gentlemen. I only want a few minutes of your time. It doesn't cost you anything to listen. Please be patient with me. I just got released from Riker's Island, where I was unjustly incarcerated for thirty days for acts I committed during a nervous breakdown due to a situation beyond my control. I am not a drug addict. This is the situation. I need your money. I could be out robbing and stealing right now. I don't want to be doing that. I could be holding a knife to your throat right now. I don't want to be doing that... And I'm sure you don't want that, either. I didn't choose this life. I want to work. But I can't. My medication costs over two thousand dollars a week, of which Medicaid only pays one-third. I am forced to go down to the Lower East Side and buy illegal drugs to stop the pain. I am not a drug addict. If you give me money, if you help me out, I might be able to find someplace to live. I might be able to get my life back together. It's really all up to you. Bad things happen to good people. Bad situations beyond my control forced me onto the streets into a life of crime. I won't bore you with the details right now. But if you don't believe me, you can call my parole officer, Mr. Vincent Bardello. His home number is 555-1768. The only difference between you and me is that you're on the ups and I'm on the downs. Underneath it all, we're exactly the same. We're both human beings. I'm a human being. I'm also a victim of a sick society. I come from a dysfunctional family. My father was an alcoholic. My mother tried to control me. My sister thinks she's an actress. You wouldn't want the childhood that I had. The world is really screwed up. Things get worse every day. Now is your chance to do something about it… help out somebody standing right in front of you instead of worrying about some skinny African ten thousand miles away. Believe me when I tell you God is watching you when you help someone less fortunate than yourself, a human being, like me. I'm sorry my clothes aren't clean. I'm sorry I'm homeless. I'm sorry I don't have a job. I'm sorry I have to interrupt your afternoon. But I have no choice. I have to ask for help. I can't change my life—you can. Please, please look into your hearts and do the right thing! Thank you.

Silent No More

By Gus Edwards

HARRIS, late 20s

Harris, an African-American male in his twenties, defends himself—and other African-American males—against cold and uncaring "black sisters," who don't seem to appreciate them. There is a sense of urgency voiced in his need to address distrustful and suspicious sisters. But it is in the fierce internal struggle taking place that Harris catches a fleeting glimpse of his own tortured spirit and soul, and is finally able to confront his demons.

I agreed to going on that TV talk show because I think it's about time one of us talked back. Black brothers, I mean. Man, if you listen to all the stuff you hear about us on them shows and believe what they write about us in magazines, then you got to think that the black man is maybe the worst species of human being God ever created. Because besides all the criminal things they tell you we done and continue to do, they also tell you that we lazy, low-minded, drunk, or drugged up most of the time, and that we don't know how to treat our women. More than we don't know how to treat them, we don't even know how to see any beauty in them. You see we all walking around blind except when some white woman pass our way, I guess. I don't know. But that's what they put in the magazines. And on TV. And I'm not just talking about white people either. I'm talking about our black sisters. Some of them anyway. They the ones you see on them talk shows talking about what bad role models we are. And what a shame that is. And one that I was watching the other day, she jumped up in front of the camera and said, "Let's talk it plain, black men are dogs!" Man, the whole audience just clap their hands and shout back at her, "That's right, Sister! You telling the truth. They is dogs, every one of them!" And I sat there thinking, I ain't no dog. And I don't appreciate nobody calling me one. Especially on TV. If somebody had said that to my face I would knock them down. I don't care how big they are, or how small. I grew up respecting women and I expect them to respect me, too. My mother was a woman and I respected her. When I got to a certain age, she respected me, too. That's the way I think things should be. "Do unto others as you would have them do unto you" is the rule I grew up with. And I try to live by it. But it don't seem like too many people go by that any more. Especially when they get on TV. It's like that camera give them license to curse you, insult you, and call you any bad name they wish. And you, 'cause you're a man, ain't supposed to say nothing about it. You supposed to take it quietly and keep your mouth shut. I mean, those people assassinating your character to a million people and you ain't supposed to say a thing except to agree. And maybe stand up in front of everybody like they do at AA meetings and say, "My name is So-and-So. I am a black man. Therefore, I am a dog." I don't think so. And I ain't doing it. Hell, no. In fact, I'm doing just the opposite. I'm going on that TV show and let the world hear my side of things. And when I do, I ain't gonna be speaking for every black man. I'm going to be speaking just for me. The rest of them don't want to talk, that's their business. I know for me, I just don't want to be silent no more.

Suburban Redux

By Andrew Biss

TRISTRAM, late teens, early 20s
From *Suburban Redux*

> *Tristram—a rather shy, awkward young man with a slightly
> off-center sense of humor—has just been rebuffed by the
> high-spirited woman he adores and, in his insecurity and
> self-loathing, places the blame upon himself for the breakup.
> Here he defines his own weaknesses. He lacks the personal
> courage or strength of character to join the struggle to
> reclaim the woman he adores, and appears content with his
> own self-centered needs. Tristram's misadventures are as
> timeless and touching as frustrated love itself.*

No, no, it's quite alright. And it isn't self-pity, it's self-knowledge. I'm quite aware of who I am. I'm quite aware that I've never had a particularly interesting or revealing thing to say or contribute in my entire life. And you needn't be kind. I—I'm not in need of sympathy. Self-knowledge is a source of strength if one's able to embrace it. But the fact remains, when you get right down to it, I'm a decidedly dull individual, and it was stupid and vain of me to imagine you could regard me as anything else. But it's who I am. I don't wish to be dull. Who would? I can imagine nothing more wonderful than to be an object of fascination in the eyes of another. But no matter how I try, it's not to be—not for me, at least. But, you see, unlike your husband, whenever I look in the mirror I'm more than capable of facing the truth—however sobering. *(Pause.)* Oh, don't get me wrong—I—I'm not saying I don't find *life* interesting. I do. I find it immeasurably interesting, as I do people, and art, and music and literature… and you. I think that must be why I love you—and love being with you as much as I do. You fill in the bits of me that are missing. When I'm with you I feel as though I *am* interesting and witty and clever. And I'm sure any number of psychologists would be happy to tell me that that's vicarious and weak and wrong of me, but you see... it makes me so very happy. But with you, as with the arts, I'm simply a receptacle for someone else's abilities. I absorb them, I feed on them, they enrich me, but at the end of the day... I bring nothing to the table.

Voices in Conflict

By Bonnie Dickinson

BRIAN, mid- to late-20s
From *Voices in Conflict* (Playscripts, Inc.)

> *Brian Mockenhaupt, a young veteran of the Iraq war, takes
> a hard look at his deployment in this piece. He reflects on
> what he saw and what he did based on his true experiences...
> and in his own words. The language here is uniquely telling,
> and the underlying pathos and sorrow shine through. This
> is real talk from a real character, describing real situations
> and relationships forged over time, and while under fire.
> It is a strong personal testament to courage and sacrifice,
> with less bravado than anticipated and more compassion
> than expected.*

I've spent hours taking in the world through a rifle scope,
watching life unfold. Women hanging laundry on a rooftop.
Men haggling over a hindquarter of lamb in the market. Children
walking to school. I've watched this and hoped that someday
I would see that my presence had made their lives better, a
redemption of sorts. But I also peered through the scope waiting
for someone to do something wrong, so I could shoot him.
When you pick up a weapon with the intent of killing, you step
onto a very strange and serious playing field. Every morning
someone wakes wanting to kill you. When you walk down the
street, they are waiting, and you want to kill them, too. That's
not bloodthirsty. That's just the trade you've learned. And as an
American soldier, you have a very impressive toolbox. You can
fire your rifle or lob a grenade, and if that's not enough, call in
the tanks, or helicopters, or jets. The insurgents have their skill
sets, too, turning mornings at the market into chaos, crowds into
scattered flesh, Humvees into charred scrap. You're all part of
the terrible magic show, both powerful and helpless. I miss Iraq.
I miss my gun. I miss my war.

Chapter 7:
Birds of a Feather

Sometimes it takes an encounter with something non-human or otherworldly to shed light on the human condition. In these monologues, animals, supernatural beings, aliens, or fantastic or legendary characters have a role in holding up a distorted, sometimes disturbing, mirror to life.

Some of the monologues consist of a character describing a fateful encounter with an extraordinary entity. Others depict the actual characters themselves, presenting their unusual perspective as commonplace. Some are humorous, others are cynical, ironic, or even lyrical.

Three of the monologues describe human encounters with the animal kingdom, describing how the animals are worse off for the attention. The speakers are well aware of the suffering humans have caused, which has given them a bitter or pessimistic view of people. Mankind is out of step with nature, disrupting a delicate balance, but the speaker is powerless to change anything. In contrast to these three monologues, another takes the point of view of an actual wolf who seeks a human ally to help rectify mankind's abuses against nature.

The callous insensitivity and barbarity of men, in contrast to aliens and the legendary Bigfoot, is depicted in two monologues. In a third, a boy earnestly relates witnessing an actual werewolf attack, knowing that his veracity will be doubted.

Fantastic characters inspired by fairy tales, children's stories, or weird fiction, but given a contemporary twist, comprise the rest of the monologues. These provide opportunities for over-the-top, exaggerated performance, but be careful to root any histrionics in clearly defined, well-developed characters. Even if an actor uses these monologues to audition for a more theatrical or presentational role, including children's theatre, musical comedy, or farce, these monologues should be played straight.

Aliens, 3 Miles, Turn Left

By Stephen A. Schrum

MAN, late 30s

Alone in his living room cluttered with pizza boxes, beer bottles, and other signs of a bachelor's lifestyle, the man talks about a surreal encounter with aliens last spring in his backyard. This is a startling (and sobering) battle cry for humanity—if you believe this clever and intriguing tale— or it's just a whimsical fable told by a man with a vivid imagination who refuses to face reality. The rather simple story examines some universal themes like freedom and hope, oppression and survival—all making serious points in a satiric manner.

And then, one night last spring, They came. I was just coming home from one of our poker nights, and it was pretty late. As I came up the driveway, I saw something out in the field. There was this weird greenish light. I didn't know what it could be, so I turned off the truck and drifted to a stop. I also pulled out my rifle I keep in the gun rack, and I snuck out to the field. And there I saw it. Right then, I knew it was all true. I'd read about it in the *National Enquirer* and the *Weekly World News*, but here it was right in front of me. Space aliens. There were three of them, about four or five feet tall, with long arms and legs, wearing some strange clothes, with these funny helmets, that looked sorta familiar but I couldn't quite figure it out. They were walking around outside their ship, picking up rocks and weeds and stuff and checking them out with some kind of small box they had, just like on *(Mispronounces.) Star Track*. But they didn't see me. They just kept on doing what they were doing, and I just kept watching them moving around, picking up rocks and weeds and stuff. After a couple of minutes, two of them walked over to the ship and start staring at some kind of crystal thing, and it starts turning purple. It was the weirdest thing, them just holding this big crystal and it starts glowing. This was kind of interesting, so I just kept watching them staring at this thing. Then all of a sudden, out of the corner of my right eye, I see that the third one is standing next to me, staring at me, and he's got some kind of little box pointed right at me. Hell, I don't know if it's a gun or what, so I take the butt of my rifle and I knock it out of his hands. But he doesn't do anything, he just stands there, staring at me with these big weird eyes. And then I hear footsteps, and I look over and the other two are running toward us, and the crystal's glowing brighter, and I figure I'm in some kind of deep crap now. So I shot 'em. I shot all three of 'em. First I shot the two running at me, and then the third. I musta scared the crap out of him, 'cause he started singing, uh, some kind of high-pitched opera thing. It gave me the shivers! So I shot him too. Man, that was weird. It was easier than shooting deer. I just shot 'em. So there I am, out in this field, with three dead aliens and an alien spaceship. And I'm trying to figure out what to do next. And then it hits me. I gotta hide this. I mean, I read these articles about when people call the government about crashed ships, and they come in and take it all away and you can't even prove that it really happened. And everybody thinks you're nuts.

Bigfoot Stole My Wife

By Ron Carlson

HUSBAND, 30s
From *The News of the World* (W.W. Norton & Co.)

This darkly comic monologue describes the problematic relationship of an estranged husband and wife, with the husband's growing realization and resigned acceptance of the callous manner in which he has treated his wife over the years.

The problem, as I'm finding out over the last few weeks, is basic credibility. A lot of people look at me and say, sure, Rick, Bigfoot stole your wife. It makes me sad to see it, the look of disbelief in each person's eye. Trudy's disappearance makes me sad, too, and I'm sick in my heart about where she may be and how he's treating her, what they do all day, if she's getting enough to eat. I believe he's being good to her—I mean I feel it—and I'm going to keep hoping to see her again, but it is my belief that I probably won't. In the two and a half years we were married, I often had the feeling that I would come home from the track and something would be funny. Oh, she'd say things: "One of these days I'm not going to be here when you get home," things like that, things like everybody says. How stupid of me not to see them as omens. When I'd get out of bed in the early afternoon, I'd stand right here at this sink and I could see her working in her garden in her cut-off Levis and bikini top, weeding, planting, watering. I mean it was obvious. I was too busy thinking about the races, weighing the odds, checking the jockey roster to see what I now know—he was watching her too. He'd probably been watching her all summer. So, in a way it was my fault. But what could I have done? Bigfoot steals your wife. I mean—even if you're home, it's going to be a mess. He's big and not well trained.

Bird in the Hand #1

By Jorge Ignacio Cortinas

FELIX, aged 27
From *Bird in the Hand* (Dramatic Publishing)

In this deftly ironic portrait of Felix, a bumbling tour guide at Birdland Family Theme Park, we have a poignant portrait of the captive flamingos. What surfaces is an acute awareness of their stress in captivity and how they are forever trapped in an unnatural, man-made world from which there is no escape—and where truth and illusion become almost inseparably entangled in a real life game of cat and mouse. In the end, there are no facile answers for these flamingos— just the hope of a future touched, at last, with some fleeting promise of freedom.

Hi and, yeah, welcome to the Flamingo exhibit. These flamingos you see here today are so out of place, so far from their native ecology, that um, they've started dying off. Enjoy them while you can. You may want to take a few pictures before they go extinct. I mean, my father is going to have to pay for my college tuition and you tourists are clearly willing to pay for admission and the birds are going to die eventually so it's not like it's anyone's fault. Every once in a while, and if we're lucky maybe they'll do it today, the flamingos start to squawk. They start running back and forth—you watch them you swear something is about to happen. They say if you see a flock of flamingos flying it looks like fireworks in the daytime—swirls of red and black feathers. I bet that looks amazing. But right in the middle of their loudest squawking—the flamingos stop. It gets so quiet afterwards, you can hear mosquitoes buzzing. Maybe the flamingos shut up when they remember—oh yeah—our wings are clipped. They could try walking, theoretically they could walk right out of here, but probably they're not sure where they would go. Probably they can't remember where they're from. Who their friends are supposed to be. Any questions?

Bird in the Hand #2

By Jorge Ignacio Cortinas

FELIX, aged 27
From *Bird in the Hand* (Dramatic Publishing)

> *Felix, a hot-blooded, fiery and darkly funny tour guide at Birdland Family Theme Park, takes you on a lively journey of the Flamingo exhibit that doesn't pull any punches. He strips away all the feel-good, speak-well veneer of a tour guide and takes a hard look at himself and what really lies beneath. Alternating sharp wit with penetrating insight, Felix paints a sobering, sometimes explosive self-portrait of himself as a funny yet frightening young man who resorts more to brooding than to reason.*

Right, so... Welcome to the Flamingo exhibit. I'm kinda hungover this morning, so if you could all keep your questions to a minimum that would be great. Sir—there will be no photography allowed today. Put the camera down, sir. Thank you. Now most people think flamingos are born pink. Actually, flamingos get their color from their food. We feed then these specially engineered food pellets—which contain this pigment that they used to get from their diet—back in the wild. And for years the food pellets worked. It kept them pink. Eventually though, homesickness catches up with you. Homesickness enters the food chain. And once it's in the food chain, how do you get it out? Specially engineered food pellets don't work anymore. Our staff biologists are working overtime on a permanent cure. Trying to get the pink back. But really, when you think about it, what do scientists know about feeling out of place? About longing? Weird because—actually—I was pretty wasted this morning, and I tried to get a few hours sleep. And I had this dream, where everyone around me speaks a foreign language. And they can't understand what I'm trying to say. I woke up suddenly. And sat up in bed and I was relieved when I realized the dream wasn't real. And then I laid back down but I couldn't get back to sleep. I was alone and wide-awake and you know— it is real. The loneliness is real.

The Boy Who Cried Werewolf

By Daniel Guyton

CHRIS, early teens
From *The Boy Who Cried Werewolf* (Pioneer Drama Service)

> *Chris, an ingenious and at times reckless youth, offers a thrilling—and challenging—dark tale to inform his classmates about the werewolf that he saw last night. Although you may have some reservations about the incident, the tale itself is quite extraordinary. The rather provocative misadventure is a genuine moment of humor that prompts laugh-out-loud surprises—and could be a funny, frenetic audition piece.*

I saw one last night. I was in my room doing my homework, and I heard a dog howling, or at least I thought it was a dog. But when I looked out my window, I saw the dog standing on his hind legs! And he was wearing a bowling shirt and pants, and he had a hat on that said Nike on it. Or… maybe it was Mike? I couldn't really see it. But anyways, he looked like a man kinda, but… really hairy. Kinda like your dad, Benny, but… younger and skinnier, I think. Anyway, his clothes were ripped, and his eyes were really yellow, and he had teeth… like really long teeth. Like the way a dog's teeth look, you know, and… and then he saw me. He looked right at me, and my whole body went numb. And then he snarled, and it looked like he wanted to eat me. I wanted to run, but I couldn't move. I just stared right at him. And that's when he howled. It was the loudest sound I have ever heard in my life, and my entire room shook. It even broke the glass on my iPad. So I ran as fast as I could down the hall into my mom's room, but my mom wasn't there. I called out to her, and that's when I heard the window break in my bedroom. So I immediately crawled under my mom's bed! I kept expecting someone to grab my leg, or to bite me or to rip me to pieces! But then everything went quiet. The noises all stopped for what

131

seemed like forever. And that's when I heard screaming. It was my neighbor, Mrs. London. She was yelling that someone ate her cat. Yelling over and over again, "Someone ate my cat! Someone ate my cat!" It was horrible. When I finally looked out my mom's window, I saw Mrs. London standing there, yelling. But the dog, or... man, or whatever, wasn't there. But it wasn't a dog at all, you guys. It was... it was a werewolf.

Brumbly the Elf

By Wade Bradford

BRUMBLY, ageless
From *Brumbly at the North Pole*

> *Even Santa's elves need an orientation session for the Christmas holiday countdown! Here, Inspector Brumbly, Senior Elf Number 8425, delivers his annual orientation lecture. He is a professional charmer, direct and playful, amusing and occasionally ironic, and yet forceful in his inspiring call to action. Inspector Brumbly's orientation session is a delightful and biting satire crammed full with earthy humor. It takes the reader on a magical journey that is itself a celebration of the holiday.*

All right, you North Pole newbies, this is your orientation. The Christmas countdown is ticking away, we don't have much time, so prick up those pointy ears and listen up! My name is Inspector Brumbly, Elf Number 8425. I have delivered this orientation speech for over a thousand years, so if I look burnt out, it is not your imagination. The number one rule here at Santa's workshop is, "When the fat man is on the floor, look busy." Everything after that is easy. As you can see, this is the main room where all of the magic happens. Make sure when you are working alongside the conveyor belt you do not wear jingle bell sleeves. Last year, Happy the Elf lost an arm. Not so happy any more. Over here, we have the stables. Yes, the reindeer fly. But their poop falls to the ground, just like the rest of us, so you can expect to be on "nugget-patrol" for the first few weeks. And if Sneaky the Elf offers you fudge from the stables, do yourself a favor and say "No, thank you." Some basic tips, common sense really. Don't stare at Rudolph's nose. He hates that. It's red. Get over it. If you see a disoriented talking snowman that says "Happy Birthday," just smile and nod politely. He's senile but harmless. Don't listen to rumors about Mrs. Claus and the Easter Bunny, and don't mention those rumors to Santa—and especially don't mention them to him after he's had more than two glasses of eggnog. Trust me on this one. I know from experience. All right, elves, that's about it. Let's get to work!

Humpty Dumpty, Private Egg

By D. M. Larson

HUMPTY DUMPTY, an egg, no longer fresh
From *Holka Polka*

Humpty Dumpty, the English nursery rhyme character, has been part of popular culture since being featured in Lewis Carroll's Through the Looking Glass. Humpty Dumpty was also a common nickname used in the fifteenth century to describe large or overweight men. Here, in this modern interpretation, Humpty Dumpty appears as a hard-boiled detective fighting evil and injustice in Fairy Tale Land, and introduces an unexpected and striking conclusion to the tale.

It was a dark and stormy night in Fairy Tale Land. A night just perfect for witches. With Fairy Godmother in the clink, I began to wonder if we were ready for a world turned topsy-turvy. Sweet witches and friendly wolves. Wise wizards and princesses with pig noses. It's a world gone mad, but somehow things are looking sunny-side up and we may find some kind of happily ever after in Fairy Tale Land. I was about to call it a day because I had this over-easy feeling coming over me… when *she* rolled in. She had the figure of a fortress and the countenance of a cobra. She was the goddaughter—the witchiest woman west of the Walla Walla. I wondered if this was some kind of yolk. I had already cracked the case of the sleeping prince. Fairy Godmother was left with egg on her face. The sleeping spell was only the Easter coloring on a much more rotten egg. She had bigger eggs to fry. And the corruption nearly broke Fairy Tale Land apart. Thankfully, they had me to put it back together again. I could continue walking on eggshells around her like everyone else, or I could put all my eggs in one basket and say it straight. I knew she was trouble and I told her so. I told her she was like one of those riddles that scramble your brains. Like "What came first, the chicken or the egg?" I told her to beat it unless she wanted to have a talk with all the king's horses and all the king's men. But then her eyes teared up and I was speechless, because I'd never seen this cool egg crack before. Hey, I've got feelings. I'm a bit soft-boiled around the dames. And this dame needed help. And help is what I do, because I'm… Humpty Dumpty, Private Egg. Hard-boiled detective.

Invisible Man

By Stacey Lane

INVISIBLE MAN, 20s or 30s
From *Can't Count on Dracula*

> *In this brief but deftly comic monologue, the Invisible Man
> quickly rises to a crisis point as he sits at the table of a
> twenty-four-hour pancake house with his friends Dracula
> and Frankenstein, lamenting how difficult it has become
> to intimidate today's young adults. Deeply personal and
> exceedingly honest, the Invisible Man isn't angry—he's
> just neurotic and thinks that he may be about to crash and
> burn if he and his creature friends lose their relevance or
> squander their "talents" for diabolical deeds in today's fast-
> food culture.*

You see, that is a perfect example. That is precisely why I called
you to this meeting, Dracula and Frankenstein. It's infuriating.
No one takes us seriously anymore. We can't even scare an old
lady. Plus, our numbers are dwindling. The Headless Horseman
has given up riding. He just sits at home and knits scarves. The
Mummy moved back in with his mommy. And the Abominable
Snowman, well, global warming has all but done him in. The
Blob has gone on a diet—he's avoiding all carbs—carbon-life
forms that is. The world used to tremble in fear, but now…
Mmm. Kids today with their violent video games, 3D movies,
and "don't be afraid of the monster under the bed" picture books.
Well, quite frankly, it's become a lot harder to scare them than
it used to be. But I will terrify them all. I will terrify every last
man, woman, and child! I'll show them that the scariest thing of
all is the one that they never see coming!

137

Lord Grinch

By Evan Guilford-Blake

LORD GRINCH, age of performer
From *True Magic* (Playscripts)

> *Lord Grinch represents the "anti-holiday" spirit of Christmas-time celebrations. He is a furry recluse living in seclusion on a cliff overlooking a cheerful, optimistic town. He scorns the Christmas season and the boisterous festivities customarily celebrated during the holidays. In this revealing confession, Lord Grinch recalls an incident in his childhood that helped define his subsequent jealousy and resentment of the holidays and shaped his unhappy destiny.*

People ask me why am I like this? *Why*? I'll tell you! Because... of... Christmas! When I was eleven, I got the best Christmas present in the world! A bright red fire truck—just like my daddy rode on. And I went outside right away, and I was vrooming with my new truck, up and down the driveway. *(Acts it out.)* Vroom, vrooooommmmm. And I was having so much fff, fff, fff—fun—just going back and forth, up and down. And it was a beautiful Christmas day, very warm, the sun was bright and there wasn't a cloud for miles. And there I was with my shiny new red truck, just—vrrooommm, vrrooommm, vrrooommm... And I let it go, and it *ran*, fast, faster, faster, like a race car, down the driveway and into the... street. And this big dump truck was coming along and I didn't see it and it—ran over my shiny new red fire truck and—*squashed it*—flat as a new dollar bill. And I took it back into the house and showed it to my mother and father, but they said we couldn't afford to replace it and that I'd have to wait till next year for Santa to bring me one. And I was a good boy, all year. I cleaned my room and I brushed my teeth and I even ate my broccoli, and then I wrote Santa a letter asking for just two things—a bicycle and a new fire truck. And I *got* the bicycle, but, but the truck never came. Not that year, not ever. And I really, *really* wanted the truck more than anything else in the whole world. And so I—stopped sending letters, and being nice and having fff, fff, fff—fun, and I wanted to make a lot of money so I could buy all the trucks I wanted. But I could never find another one just like the one daddy rode on... So, now I'm *(Actor's age.)* and the whole darn world thinks I'm Mr. Grinch. Well, too bad! I'm not—I'm Lord Grinch to you, and if you don't like it you can take a long vrroom off a short driveway yourself!

Scotch and Donuts

By John Longenbaugh

TOM, aged 30
From *Scotch and Donuts*

> *Tom, an inquisitive and serious young man with a passion
> for adventure, enjoys trying to unravel life's contradictions
> and mysteries—especially when the challenge is as
> unconventional as studying the mating habits of lemmings!
> Here he is addressing the fact that lemmings—small
> rodents like muskrats usually found in or near the Arctic—
> are not prone to commit mass suicide as some scholars
> have suggested.*

Actually, not a lot of people know this, but lemmings don't
commit mass suicide. That's a myth. Yes, I know we've all seen
that nature movie of them leaping off cliffs into the sea. But it's
a fake. These nature photographers from Disney were told that
migrating lemmings leap off cliffs, so they grabbed their cameras
and headed off to the fjords. Trouble was, once they got there,
the lemmings wouldn't cooperate. So they "assisted them." A
couple of the guys stood on a cliff with a pen full of lemmings
and tossed the little rodents into the sea below while their friend
filmed. It was a nature snuff film. Then, there's the irony of that
narrator's voice asking, "Will we ever learn what mysterious
force drives these animals to their death?" But I think, more
to the point, will lemmings ever learn what mysterious force
drives a bunch of filmmakers to toss their hapless little bodies
over a cliff? I used to think the lemming story taught us about
the natural urge toward self-destruction. But all it really does is
hold the mirror up to us.

The Wolf's Resolve

By Robin Rice Lichtig

WOLF, adult
From *Frontier*

The evening is aglow with a true satirist's affectionate regard for the very folly that is laid bare here: a male wolf with human attributes searches to find a human being with sensitivity to help decipher the signs of impending doom. Instantly engaging and deeply provocative, this memorable monologue stuns with the power of haunting simplicity. This evocative piece is both a social satire and a compelling character portrait.

My mission involves a lot of travel. Bus, car, train… Train is best. Confined enough to get to know them, but not so confined I can't leap off as needed. I don't travel in vans. Not anymore. It started with a man—a man who loved wolves. He found us deep in the wilderness, far to the north. Three of us climbed in his van. We went with him seeking adventure. We were very young. The man drove the van to towns. He took us to schools and auditoriums to teach people about us. It was strange, being inside. Strange sounds bouncing off hard, inside walls. Strange smells. He had to coax us to come out on stage. We let people pat us and hold our paws and lift our lips to look at our teeth. One day he took us to New York City in his van. He parked and went into a restaurant. People pressed their faces to the van windows. They shouted for others to come see. Come see the scary wolves. A shot through the back window. Five shots and we were dead. People clapped. People laughed. The big bad wolves are dead! The faces pressed to the windows are a blur. But I remember the man. How he rubbed my ears and spoke softly. The pack wants revenge—for every wolf shot for sport, for every wolf that ever chewed off a leg to escape a trap. Revenge for men calling us evil. Revenge for poisoning children's minds with grandmother-eating, pig-baiting wolves from their sick stories. Revenge for plundering the land. But the traveling man would say, "Revenge is no reason to kill. Not if you know love." I had to separate from the pack to move ahead with my mission. On full-moon nights I ache with missing them, but I must save mankind from itself to honor that pearl of goodness in the kind man and others like him. Good must be preserved no matter how rare, no matter what the species. Mother Nature is growing impatient with how humans are treating the Earth. She won't put up with it much longer. They must wake up. This is my mission. I need to find a human with sensitivity to signs of impending doom. Signs like a loon with eyes as red as fire, an eagle circling counter-clockwise. A harvest mouse running toward a jungle cat. This human will recognize signs and warn the others. I'm looking for a woman. Perhaps an artist. Artists are exceptionally aware of the ebb and flow of nature. She'll be on a train, I'm quite sure. She'll be sitting by a window where she can see the passing landscape. Mountains torn with mining, fields laid waste with chemicals, rivers choked with pollution, forests scarred by fire. She'll have wiped a clean circle on the window with her handkerchief and pressed her nose against the glass. When she sees a sign, tears will run down her cheeks, but she'll be silent because she'll be married to a man who has wrapped her in false security—thrown a bucket of water on the fire in her belly. She will have backed away, shut her eyes, burrowed into a small life to feel safe. This woman dreams of standing on the crest of a mountain with words of warning streaming from her mouth. But caring for the man and his babies has consumed her. I will find her. I will be there on the train, on the seat beside her. I'll take hold of her shoulder and turn her to look in my eyes. She'll be frightened. "No, no. I can't do anything. I'm only one," she'll say. But my eyes will hold her. She can't escape. She'll see the what-is and the what-will-be if she doesn't act. The amber in my eyes will shift her like a continental plate. She'll see that changes must be made, and fast. She'll sound the alarm that will turn the tide for all of us. Tell me if you see this woman. Time is growing short.

Chapter 8:
Literary and Period

The monologues from this section, while not written specifically for live performance, possess narrative qualities, clearly defined characters, and dramatic arcs. These elements can make them suitable as audition pieces, but only if selections from literary sources are permitted by the director. Be sure to double check the eligibility of these materials.

The language in these monologues is somewhat heightened, but not specifically *classical*, as with a Shakespeare text. Extra attention should be given to breath control, pronunciation, and making sense of unfamiliar vocabulary and sentence structures, as these monologues are more challenging than conversational speech.

In the monologues drawn from novels, the narrating character is fully developed and requires the same preparation you would give to rehearsing a role from a play script. One requires dialect, and another consists of a series of short vignettes spaced out over a period of time. Transitions between the vignettes need to be punctuated so that the distinctions are clear in performance. The third is a contemporary translation of a nineteenth-century work, but demands significant emotional investment to communicate a disturbingly symbolic childhood memory.

The essay monologues reflect a satirical persona of the authors and their literary voices, but it is not necessary to impersonate Lamb or Swift. The style of speech and physical posture does require some characterization, as their opinions are rooted in a particular time and culture. These monologues should be performed as if giving a public lecture, earnestly and with a straight face, layering in just a hint of tongue-in-cheek irony.

Adam's Diary

By Mark Twain

ADAM, 20s
From *The Diary of Adam and Eve*

> *This comic short story written by American humorist Mark Twain is an interesting narrative monologue selection if the audition notice does not limit material to only character monologues from play scripts. The piece is both humorous and ironic, and gives a new spin on Genesis. This excerpt focuses on the birth of Cain and Adam's struggle to identify Cain's species—initially thinking he is a fish, then a kangaroo, and then a bear. Eventually, however, Adam determines that since Cain lives and breathes... he must be a human, like himself!*

MONDAY. We have named it Cain. She caught it while I was away trapping on the North Shore of the Erie. It resembles us in some ways, and may be a close relation. That is what she thinks, but this is an error, in my judgment. The difference in size warrants that it is a different and new kind of animal—a fish, perhaps, although when I put it in the water to see, it sank, and she plunged in and snatched it out before there was an opportunity to determine the matter. WEDNESDAY. It isn't a fish. It makes curious noises when not satisfied, and says "goo goo" when it is. It is not one of us, for it doesn't walk. THREE MONTHS LATER. I sleep but little. It has ceased lying around, and goes about on its four legs now. Yet it differs from the other four-legged animals in that its front legs are unusually short; consequently causing the main part of the person to stick up uncomfortably high in the air, and this is not attractive. FOUR MONTHS LATER. The kangaroo still continues to grow. It has fur on his head now, except that it is much finer and softer, and instead of being black, it's red. FIVE MONTHS LATER. The bear has learned to paddle around all by itself on its hind legs, and says "poppa" and "momma!" It is certainly a new species.

I will go off on a far expedition among the forests of the north and make an exhaustive search. There must certainly be another one somewhere, and this one will be less dangerous when it has company of its own species. In my judgment, it is either an enigma or some kind of bug. THREE MONTHS LATER. It has been a weary hunt, and I have had no success. In the meantime, without stirring from the home estate she has caught another one! I never saw such luck. This new one is as ugly now as the old one was at first, has the same sulphur and raw meat complexion and the same singular head without any fur on it… She calls it Abel. TEN YEARS LATER. They are boys! We found it out long ago. It was their coming in that small shape that puzzled us. There are some girls now. Abel is a good boy, but if Cain had stayed a bear it would have improved him.

A Bachelor's Complaint of the Behavior of Married People

By Charles Lamb

BACHELOR, 30s

> *This non-dramatic, satiric essay by Charles Lamb is a fun piece to perform in a classroom setting or in an audition if the notice does not specifically indicate that material must be selected from contemporary play scripts. Written in 1865, the author details his bitter experiences with the behavior of married people who still pretend to be lovers, prefer the company of one another to all others, and shamelessly flaunt their love in the face of single people. The author also offers a sense of hilarity that belies his deep concerns.*

As a single man, I have spent a good deal of my time in noting down the infirmities of married people, to console myself for those superior pleasures which they tell me I have lost by remaining single as I am. I cannot say that the quarrels of men and their wives ever made any great impression upon me. What oftenest offends me is an error of quite a different description— it is that they are too *loving*. They carry their preference undisguisedly, they perk it up in the faces of us single people so shamelessly. You cannot be in their company a moment without being made to feel that you are not the object of this preference. It is enough that I know I am not. I do not want this perpetual reminding. Nothing is to me more distasteful than that entire complacency and satisfaction which beam in the countenances of a new-married couple—in that of the lady particularly. It tells you that her lot is disposed of in this world, that you can have no hopes of her. It is true, I have none. Nor wishes either, perhaps. But this is one of those truths which ought to be taken for granted, not expressed or publicly announced. And this is not the worst. If the husband be a man with whom you have lived on a friendly footing before his marriage—look about you—your tenure is precarious. Innumerable are the ways which wives take to insult and worm you out of their husband's confidence. Laughing at all you say with a kind of wonder, as if you were a strange kind of fellow that said good things, but an oddity! But what I have spoken of hitherto is nothing to the airs which these creatures give themselves when they come, as they generally do, to have children. When I consider how little of a rarity these children are, I cannot for my life tell what cause for pride there can possibly be in ever having them!

Crime and Punishment

By Marilyn Campbell and Curt Columbus

Based on the novel by Fyodor Dostoyevsky

RASKOLNIKOV, 20s
From *Crime and Punishment* (Dramatic Publishing Company)

In this translation of the classical Russian novel, the focus is on the mental anguish and moral dilemma of Rodion Raskolnikov, the impoverished ex-student in St. Petersburg who executes a plan to kill an unscrupulous pawnbroker for her cash. He commits this murder to test his own cruel hypothesis that some people are naturally capable of such things, and even have the right to do them, if they believe that murder is in pursuit of a higher and more noble purpose.

In my dream, I'm about six years old, and I'm walking with my father. It's a holiday of some kind, and it's near evening. We're on the outskirts of our town, which is all laid out in front of us like a toy-train city, running right off up to the edge of the sky. There are no trees around, for some reason, except for a little black line of forest along the horizon. That little line frightens me, so I try not to look at it. I think we are going to visit the cemetery, past the tavern, going to visit my grandmother's grave. Also the little grave next to hers that holds my younger brother, who died shortly after he was born. I was still an infant myself, so I never really knew him. I only knew that I'd been told about my younger brother, so every time we went to the cemetery, I would make the sign of the cross, very religiously and bow down and kiss the little headstone. So I'm walking with my father, when we see this crowd of people. Drunk. Singing and laughing and playing balalaikas. And in the middle of the crowd is a heavy old cart, filled with stuff, with a tired old mare strapped into the harness. She's sitting on the ground, refusing to move. Her master is a big, red-faced young man, who keeps whipping her and saying, "Climb in! She'll pull us, she's going to pull us if I have to beat her to death!" And he keeps whipping her, around the face, around the eyes, and now she's bleeding, and everyone is laughing and shouting, "Finish her! Finish the old nag!" So her master takes out a crowbar and says, "She's mine. She's my goods, I'll take care of her." And he starts to beat her, on her back, on her legs, and her face and her head and everywhere. But she won't die. She tries to pull the cart. But she can't now, with broken legs and a broken back. And he keeps swinging the crowbar, beating her into the ground. Beating her. Till there's nothing left. Nothing at all. In my dream. I'm clutching my father's hand and crying, crying so hard that I can barely see. And I say, "Father! Why did they kill her? Why did they kill the poor old horse?" And he says, "Because they're drunk, Rodya. Because they're people." *(Pause.)* "It's none of our business!" It's only a dream... It's only a dream. That's all. And I must have a fever. That's all that it is. I've done nothing. I'm fine. I've done nothing wrong. God grants peace to the dead.

Huckleberry Finn

By Mark Twain

HUCK FINN, mid-teens
From *The Adventures of Huckleberry Finn*

> *Here is a faithful and rousing retelling of Mark Twain's classic
> novel of the young rascal Huckleberry Finn and his attempt
> to escape civilization before his Aunt Sally has a chance to
> "tame" him. This monologue from the novel parallels the
> narrative from the Broadway musical* Big River *and focuses
> on Huck's spirit of reckless adventure and genuine honesty
> and compassion. The monologue may also be a companion
> piece to musical theatre auditions.*

I felt good and all washed clean of sin for the first time I had
ever felt so in my life, and I knowed I could pray now. But I
didn't do it straight off, but laid the paper down and then set
there thinking—thinking how good it was all this happened
so, and how near I come to being lost and going to hell. And
went on thinking. And got to thinking over our trip down the
river, and I see Jim before me all the time... in the day and
in the nighttime, sometimes in moonlight, sometimes storms,
and we a-floating along, talking and singing and laughing. But
somehow I couldn't seem to strike no place to harden me against
him, but only the other kind. I'd see him standing on my watch
on top of his'n, 'stead of calling me, so I could go on sleeping
and see him how glad he was when I came back out of the fog,
and when I come to him again in the swamp, up there where the
feud was, and such-like times, and would always call me honey,
and pet me, and do everything he could think of for me, and how
good he always was. And at last I struck the time I saved him by
telling the men we had smallpox aboard, and he was so grateful,
and said I was the best friend old Jim ever had in the world, and
the only one he's got now, and then I happened to look around
and see that paper. It was a close place. I took it up, and held it

in my hand. I was trembling, because I'd got to decide, forever, betwixt two things, and I knowed it. I studies a minute, sort of holding my breath, and then says to myself, "All right, then I'll go to hell"—and then tore it up.

A Modest Proposal
By Jonathan Swift

SPEAKER, 30s

Plating monologues from non-dramatic sources like novels, short stories, diaries, biographies, or other narrative sources is always challenging, but can also be a memorable audition experience. If the posted audition call does not indicate that monologues must be from published play scripts—and may be from non-dramatic sources like historical documents, original scripts, short stories, diaries, or novels, for example—you may wish to consider the following non-dramatic piece. The excerpt is from Jonathan Swift's pamphlet, "A Modest Proposal," and is a satirical essay initially published anonymously in 1792. The controversial essay suggested that the impoverished Irish might ease their economic troubles by selling their children as food for rich gentlemen and ladies in high society. Swift's essay is mocking the heartless attitudes toward the poor and downtrodden Irish in the historical period.

There are a hundred and twenty thousand children of poor parents annually born. The question, therefore, is how this number shall be reared and provided for, which as I have already said, under the present situation of affairs, is utterly impossible by all the methods hitherto proposed by our government. For we can neither employ them in handicraft or agriculture, and they can very seldom pick up a livelihood by stealing till they arrive at six years old. Although, I confess, they learn the rudiments much earlier, during which time they can however be looked upon as probationers. I shall now, therefore, humbly propose my own thoughts, which I hope will not be liable to the least objection. I have been assured by a very knowing American of my acquaintance in London, that a young healthy child well nursed is at a year old a most delicious, nourishing, and wholesome food, whether stewed, roasted, baked, or boiled. And I make no doubt that it will equally serve in a fricassee or a ragout.

I do therefore humbly offer it to public consideration that of the hundred and twenty thousand children, already computed, twenty thousand may be reserved for breed, whereof one fourth part to be males, which is more than we allow to sheep, black cattle, or swine. And my reason is that these children are seldom the fruits of marriage, a circumstance not much regarded by our savages. Therefore, one male will be sufficient to serve four females. That the remaining hundred thousand may at a year be offered in sale to the persons of some quality and fortune through the kingdom, always advising the mother to let them suck plentifully in the last month, so as to render them plump and fat for a good table. A child will make two dishes at an entertainment for friends, and when the family dines alone, the fore or hind quarter will make a reasonable dish, and seasoned with a little pepper or salt will be very good boiled on the fourth day, especially in winter. I grant that this food will be somewhat dear, and therefore very proper for landlords, who, as they have already devoured most of the parents, seem to have the best title to the children!

Copyright and Performance Rights Information

Copyright laws exist to protect the creative and intellectual property rights of creators of original works. All creative works, including monologues and scripts, are considered copyrighted. There are, however, a number of "fair use" exceptions for educational or instructional purposes related to classroom performance. The original and published audition monologues in this collection are fully protected under the copyright laws of the United States of America and of all countries covered by the International Copyright Union (including Canada and the rest of the Commonwealth of Nations), and of all countries covered by the Pan-American Copyright Convention, the Universal Copyright Convention, the Berne Convention and of all other countries with which the United States has reciprocal copyright relations. For additional information related to auditions, full-scale productions, staged readings or any performance restrictions please contact the author or the author's agent at the address listed below.

Copyright laws also exist to protect creative and intellectual property rights of authors or creators of original works that may appear in print in an abbreviated form. The original and unpublished monologues that appear in this collection remain the sole intellectual property of the authors. Please contact each of the following authors individually to update subsequent monologue or complete script publication status.

Chapter 2: A Lighter Touch

Actor! By Frederick Stroppel. Copyright © 1998 by Frederick Stroppel. Reprinted by permission of the author. For additional information, contact the author at 4 Perkins Court, Glen Cove, NY 11542.

The Bold, The Young and The Murdered by Don Zolidis. Copyright © 2013 by Don Zolidis. Reprinted by permission of the author and Playscripts, Inc. For additional information, contact Playscripts, Inc. at 7 Penn Plaza, Suite 904, New York, NY 10001.

Cheese by Eric Bogosian. Copyright © 2014 by Eric Bogosian. Reprinted by permission of the Theatre Communications Group. For additional information, contact the Theatre Communications Group at 520 Eighth Ave., 24th Floor, New York, NY 10018.

Dick by Robin Rothstein. Copyright © 2012 by Robin Rothstein. Reprinted by permission of the author and Abrams Artists Agency. For additional information, contact Abrams Artists Agency at 275 Seventh Ave., 26th Floor, New York, NY 10001.

Employees Must Wash Hands... Before Murder by Don Zolidis. Copyright © 2006 by Don Zolidis. Reprinted by permission of the author and Playscripts, Inc. For additional information, contact Playscripts, Inc. at 7 Penn Plaza, Suite 904, New York, NY 10001.

Hairball by Lindsay Price. Copyright © 2010 by Lindsay Price. Reprinted by permission of the author. For additional information, contact the author at www.theatrefolk.com.

The Hunger by Steven Korbar. Copyright © 2010 by Steven Korbar. Reprinted by permission of the author. For additional information, contact the author at stevenkorbar@gmail.com.

I Hate Math by Connie Schindewolf. Copyright © 2014 by Connie Schindewolf. Reprinted by permission of the author. For additional information, contact the author at connieschindewolf@yahoo.com.

I Know What the Guy Eats for Breakfast by Leigh Podgorski. Copyright © 2015 by Leigh Podgorski. Reprinted by permission of the author. For additional information, contact the author at leighpod@aol.com.

New Action Army by Eric Bogosian. Copyright © 2014 by Eric Bogosian. Reprinted by permission of the Theatre Communications Group. For additional information, contact the Theatre Communications Group at 520 Eighth Ave., 24th Floor, New York, NY 10018.

Till We Meet Again by Colin and Mary Crowther. Copyright © 2012 by Colin and Mary Crowther. Reprinted by permission of Samuel French Ltd. For additional information, contact Samuel French Ltd. at 52 Fitzroy Street, London W1T 5JR England, United Kingdom.

The Vandal by Hamish Linklater. Copyright © 2013 by Hamish Linklater. Reprinted by permission of ICM Partners. For additional information, contact the author's agent at ICM Partners, 730 Fifth Ave., 3rd Floor, New York, NY 10019.

Chapter 3: Guilt and Regret

All Good Children Go to Heaven by M.E.H. Lewis and Barbara Lhota. Copyright © 2015 by M.E.H. Lewis and Barbara Lhota. Reprinted by permission of the authors. For additional information, contact Barbara Lhota at barblhota@gmail.com.

Aposiopesis by John P. McEneny. Copyright © 2013 by John P. McEneny. Reprinted by permission of the author. For additional information, contact the author at 332 Fifth Street, #4R, Brooklyn, NY 11215.

Basketball Champ by Steven Fendrich. Copyright © 1999 by Pioneer Drama Service, Inc. For additional information, contact Pioneer Drama Service at PO Box 4267, Englewood, CO 80155 or www.pioneerdrama.com.

Bring Back Peter Paul Rubens by Barbara Lhota and Janet B. Milstein. Copyright © 2003 by Barbara Lhota and Janet B. Milstein. Reprinted by permission of the authors. For

Chapter 4: Tragedy and Trauma

Dad Left on Some Fast Reindeer by Michael Thomas. Copyright © 1998 by Michael Thomas. Reprinted by permission of the author. For additional information, contact the author at 106 N. Olive, Fayetteville, AR 72701.

The History of Invulnerability by David Bar Katz. Copyright © 2010 by David Bar Katz. Reprinted by permission of Washington Square Films. For additional information, contact Washington Square Films at 310 Bowery, 2nd Floor, New York, NY 10012.

Just Like I Wanted by Rebecca Schlossberg. Copyright © 2014 by Rebecca Schlossberg. Reprinted by permission of the author and Playscripts, Inc. For additional information, contact Playscripts, Inc. at 7 Penn Plaza, Suite 904, New York, NY 10001.

My Room by Charles Belov. Copyright © 2015 by Charles Belov. Reprinted by permission of the author. For additional information, contact the author at PO Box 190188, San Francisco, CA 94119.

Pictures on the Internet by Daniel Guyton. Copyright © 2013 by Daniel Guyton. Reprinted by permission of the author and JAC Publishing & Promotions. For additional information, contact the author at www.danguyton.com.

Rabbit Hole by David Lindsay-Abaire. Copyright © 2006 by David Lindsay-Abaire. Reprinted by permission of the Theatre Communications Group. For additional information, contact the Theatre Communications Group at 520 Eighth Ave., 24th Floor, New York, NY 10018.

Real Life developed by Christopher P. Nichols, David Marquis, and the students of 2nd Chance Productions. Copyright © 1996. Reprinted by permission of David Marquis. For additional information, contact David Marquis at 3110 W. Kiest Boulevard, Dallas, TX 75233.

Thank You for Flushing My Head in the Toilet by Jonathan Dorf. Copyright © 2006 by Jonathan Dorf. Reprinted by permission of the author and Playscripts, Inc. For additional information, contact Playscripts, Inc. at 7 Penn Plaza, Suite

904, New York, NY 10001.

You Been Lied To by Barbara Lhota and Janet B. Milstein. Copyright © 2003 by Barbara Lhota and Janet B. Milstein. Reprinted by permission of the authors. For additional information, contact the authors at barblhota@gmail.com.

Chapter 5: Hope and Gratitude

The Art Room by Billy Aronson. Copyright © 2012 by Billy Aronson. Reprinted by permission of the author and Broadway Play Publishing. For additional information, contact Broadway Play Publishing at 224 East 62nd Street, New York, NY 10065.

Bob: A Life in Five Acts by Peter Sinn Nachtrieb. Copyright © 2013 by Peter Sinn Nachtrieb. Reprinted by permission of the author and Bret Adams Limited Artists Agency. For additional information, contact the author's agent at 448 West 44th Street, New York, NY 10036.

Grandpa by Steven Bergman. Copyright © 2005 by Steven Bergman. Reprinted by permission of the author. For additional information, contact the author at EAHINC@comcast.net.

God in Bed by Glenn Alterman. Copyright © 2015 by Glenn Alterman. Reprinted by permission of the author. For additional information, contact the author at 400 West 43rd Street, #7G, New York, NY 10036.

Moonboy by Aoise Stratford. Copyright © 2012 by Aoise Stratford. Reprinted by permission of the author. For additional information, contact the author at aoise@hotmail.com, or the author's agent Patricia McLaughlin, Beacon Artists Agency, at beaconagency@hotmail.com.

My Brother Adam by Amanda Kozik. Copyright © 2015 by Amanda Kozik. Reprinted by permission of the author. For additional information, contact the author at amandakozik@yahoo.com.

The Messenger by Eric Bogosian. Copyright © 2014 by Eric Bogosian. Reprinted by permission of the Theatre

Communications Group. For additional information, contact the Theatre Communications Group at 520 Eighth Ave., 24th Floor, New York, NY 10018.

Rat King by Troy Diana and James Valetti. Copyright © 2008 by Troy Diana and James Valletti. Reprinted by permission of the authors. For additional information, contact the authors at 1231 Randolph Road, Plainfield, NJ 07060.

The Wastes of Time by Duncan Pflaster. Copyright © 2006 by Duncan Pflaster. Reprinted by permission of the author. For additional information, contact the author at himself@ duncanpflaster.com.

Chapter 6: Outsiders

Advice to the Players by Bruce Bonafede, Copyright © 2014 by Bruce Bonafede. Reprinted by permission of the author and Samuel French, Inc. For additional information, contact Samuel French Inc. at info@samuelfrench.com.

Blacktop Sky by Christina Anderson. Copyright © 2013 by Christina Anderson. Reprinted by permission of the author and Bret Adams Limited Artists Agency. For additional information, contact the author's agent at 448 West 44th Street, New York, NY 10036.

Dream of a Deer at Dusk by Adam Kraar. Copyright © 2014 by Adam Kraar. Reprinted by permission of the author. For additional information, contact the author's agent at Elaine Devlin Literary, Inc. at 411 Lafayette Street, 6th Floor, New York, NY 10003 or edevlinlit@aol.com.

Good Mourning, America by Lucy Wang. Copyright © 2015 by Lucy Wang. Reprinted by permission of the author. For additional information, contact the author at Ard Eevin Ave., Glendale, CA 91202.

Matthew by Aino Sofia Dubrawsky. Copyright © 2015 by Aino Sofia Dubrawsky. Reprinted by permission of the author. For additional information, contact the author at ainosofia@ aim.com.

My Superpower by Lucy Wang. Copyright © 2013 by Lucy

Chapter 7: Birds of a Feather

robinricenyc@gmail.com.

Chapter 8: Literary and Period

Adam's Diary by Mark Twain. Adapted by Gerald Lee Ratliff © 2010. In *An Introduction to Reader's Theatre* (Pioneer Drama Service, Inc.). For additional information, contact Pioneer Drama Service at PO Box 4267, Englewood, CO 80155 or www.pioneerdrama.com.

Crime and Punishment translated by Marilyn Campbell and Curt Columbus. Copyright © 2006 by Marilyn Campbell and Curt Columbus. Reprinted by permission of Dramatic Publishing and the authors. For additional information, contact Marilyn Campbell at marilyncampbell@gmail.com.

About the Editors

Gerald Lee Ratliff is an award-winning author of numerous articles and textbooks in classroom teaching strategies and performance activities. He has served as national president of the Eastern Communication Association, Association of Communication Administration, and Theta Alpha Phi, the national theatre fraternity. He was awarded the Distinguished Service Award by both the Eastern Communication Association and Theta Alpha Phi, named a Fulbright Scholar to China, selected as a U.S.A. delegate of the John F. Kennedy Center for the Performing Arts to Russia, and has received multiple teaching awards for pioneering innovative curriculum design and instructional practices. He is currently active as a program consultant and frequent workshop facilitator.

Patrick Rainville Dorn has an MA in Theatre from the University of Denver. He taught English and drama at Colorado Christian University, wrote and directed plays for Colorado ACTS, and has more than forty published plays. As a theatre critic, he has written hundreds of reviews for a daily newspaper and his own blog, and also writes children's books and fiction. Check out his website at: www.patrickdorn.com.